Behind Palace Walls: Uncovering The Truth About British Royalty

Dhulia Bharat

Published by Dhulia Bharat, 2024.

While every precaution has been taken in the preparation of this book, the publisher assumes no responsibility for errors or omissions, or for damages resulting from the use of the information contained herein.

BEHIND PALACE WALLS: UNCOVERING THE TRUTH ABOUT BRITISH ROYALTY

First edition. May 17, 2024.

ISBN: 979-8224741151

Written by Dhulia Bharat.

Table of Contents

Chapter 1: The History of British Royalty

THE ORIGINS OF THE Monarchy

The concept of monarchy can be traced back to the earliest civilizations known to man. In these nascent societies, political power often rested in the hands of tribal elders or prominent individuals who possessed qualities deemed essential for leadership, such as strength, intelligence, or charisma. With the passage of time, these leaders began to consolidate their power and establish hereditary lines of succession, giving birth to the concept of monarchy.

One of the earliest examples of monarchy can be found in ancient Mesopotamia. The Sumerian civilization, which emerged around 4000 BCE in the region that is now modern-day Iraq, provides valuable insights into the origins of monarchy. The Sumerians created a highly complex society with urban centers, sophisticated legal systems, and elaborate religious rituals. Within this multifaceted society, the role of the king, or "lugal," emerged as a central figure.

The Sumerian monarchy was not a purely autocratic system but was rather rooted in a system of divine kingship. The king was believed to be a mortal representative of the gods, endowed with divine authority to rule over the people and ensure prosperity and order. This religious aspect of monarchy conferred legitimacy and divine sanction upon the ruler, bolstering their power and solidifying their position within society.

The ancient Egyptians, too, developed a unique form of monarchy that endured for thousands of years. The pharaoh, a term derived from the Egyptian word "per-aa," meaning "great house," held supreme authority and was considered both a political and divine figure. Like the Sumerian rulers, the pharaohs were believed to be direct descendants of the gods, further reinforcing their status as the embodiment of divine power on Earth.

The pharaohs wielded absolute political authority and were responsible for maintaining the cosmic order, or "ma'at," in Egyptian society. They governed with the assistance of a complex bureaucracy and relied heavily on religious rituals and ceremonies to solidify their rule. The concept of the pharaoh as an intermediary between the mortal and divine worlds became deeply ingrained in Egyptian culture, ensuring the continuity of the monarchy for centuries.

Moving beyond the ancient Near East, the Greco-Roman world offers another fascinating perspective on the origins of monarchy. In Greece, the concept of monarchy began to give way to alternative forms of governance, such as oligarchy and democracy. However, the Hellenistic period saw the rise of powerful monarchies, notably the Macedonian Empire under the reign of Alexander the Great.

Alexander's conquests and subsequent establishment of an expansive empire set the stage for the rise of Hellenistic monarchies. These monarchies were characterized by a fusion of Greek and eastern traditions, resulting in a unique blend of political systems. The monarchs, known as "hellenistic kings," adopted the title of "basileus," derived from the Greek word for king, reinforcing their authority and connecting themselves to the ancient Greek tradition of monarchy.

The monarchies of the Hellenistic period drew inspiration from both the divine kingship of the Near East and the ideals of Greek political philosophy. The rulers sought to legitimize their power by associating themselves with Greek cultural values, sponsoring the arts, and cultivating alliances with Greek city-states. This fusion of political power and cultural influence allowed the Hellenistic monarchies to flourish for several centuries. From ancient Mesopotamia to Egypt, Greece, and beyond, various societies championed the concept of monarchy, albeit with different nuances and cultural variations. Whether rooted in divine kingship, political authority, or a fusion of both, the institution of monarchy played a significant role in shaping the course of human history. By understanding the origins of monarchy, we can gain valuable insights into the evolution of political systems and appreciate the complex dynamics that have shaped our modern world.

The Evolution of the Royal Family

To understand the evolution of the royal family, one must delve into its historical roots. The British monarchy traces its ancestry back over a thousand years, with kings and queens ruling the land since the early medieval period. The monarchy has faced numerous challenges and upheavals throughout its existence, including invasions, civil wars, revolutions, and shifts in political power. Despite these uncertainties, the royal family has managed to survive and evolve, adapting to changing circumstances and societal expectations.

One pivotal period in the evolution of the royal family occurred during the Tudor dynasty's reign in the 16th century. The Tudors, particularly Henry VIII and his daughter, Elizabeth I, played a significant role in transforming the monarchy into a more centralised and powerful institution. This era witnessed the establishment of the Church of England and the solidification of the monarch's authority over religious matters. The Tudor dynasty also witnessed the rise of courtly culture and the spread of the monarchy's influence beyond the British Isles.

Another milestone in the evolution of the royal family came during the Victorian era, with Queen Victoria's reign from 1837 to 1901. Victoria's reign was marked by an expansion of the British Empire and significant advancements in industrialisation and technological innovations. This period saw the royal family embrace new forms of communication, with the advent of photography and the inauguration of the telegraph system. Queen Victoria's strong emphasis on family values and the emergence of a more accessible, relatable monarchy laid the foundations for the modern-day perception of the royals.

Perhaps the most transformative period in recent royal history was the 20th century, which witnessed unprecedented changes within the family and the monarchy as a whole. The British royal family faced immense challenges during this time, including the two World Wars and changing public attitudes towards monarchy. The tumultuous abdication of King Edward VIII in 1936 further shook the institution, demonstrating the need for a more modern and adaptable monarchy. The subsequent reigns of Queen Elizabeth II and her children saw the royal family navigate its way through a rapidly changing world, from the advent of television and mass media to shifts in public sentiment towards the monarchy.

In the latter half of the 20th century, the royal family became increasingly aware of the need to modernise and connect with the public on a more personal level. The marriage of Prince Charles to Lady Diana Spencer in 1981 represented a new era for the monarchy, with Diana's charisma and relatability captivating the world. However, it also highlighted the pressures and challenges faced by individuals within the royal family and the subsequent impact on their public image.

The evolution of the royal family in the 21st century has been marked by several significant milestones. The crowning moment was undoubtedly the wedding of Prince William to Catherine Middleton in 2011, which captured the public imagination and reaffirmed the monarchy's relevance and continuity. This wedding, along with the subsequent birth of their children, Prince George, Princess Charlotte, and Prince Louis, brought a renewed sense of excitement and optimism to the British royal family.

Furthermore, the marriage of Prince Harry to Meghan Markle in 2018 signalled a significant shift in the royal family's approach to tradition and inclusivity. Meghan, as a biracial and divorced American actress, brought a fresh perspective to the institution, challenging long-held traditions and sparking important conversations about modernity and diversity within the monarchy. This evolution highlights the royal family's ability to adapt and reflect the changing times. From its origins in the medieval period to the present day, the royal family has adapted to social, political, and cultural shifts, ensuring its continued relevance and endurance. The Tudor dynasty's centralisation of power, Queen Victoria's emphasis on family values, and the royal family's modernisation throughout the 20th and 21st centuries have all played vital roles in shaping the monarchy we see today. As we look towards the future, the evolution of the royal family will undoubtedly continue, guided by the necessity to remain connected, relatable, and responsive to the world around them.

Chapter 2: The Role of the Monarchy in Modern Society

THE ROYAL FAMILY'S Cultural Significance

Historical tradition undoubtedly underpins the cultural significance of the Royal Family. The monarchy's roots can be traced back over a thousand years, and throughout this vast expanse of time, it has weathered countless challenges and transitions. This enduring institution provides a sense of continuity, stability, and familiarity, serving as a symbolic anchor in the face of a rapidly changing world. The ceremony and pomp associated with royal engagements, such as the State Opening of Parliament and the Changing of the Guard, offer a glimpse into a bygone era that appeals to our fascination with history and tradition. As custodians of a rich and storied past, the Royal Family represents a connection to the nation's collective heritage, evoking a sense of pride and nostalgia.

Global visibility is another key element that contributes to the cultural significance of the Royal Family. The media's extensive coverage of royal events ensures that the monarchy is a constant presence in the public eye, both within the United Kingdom and across the world. From royal weddings and births to state visits and charitable endeavors, the Royal Family commands attention on a global stage, capturing the imaginations of millions. Their carefully curated image as ambassadors of British culture and values projects an aspirational and glamorous lifestyle that is often romanticized. In turn, this visibility enhances the Royal Family's cultural impact, generating curiosity and intrigue while also fostering a sense of accessibility and relatability.

Moreover, the Royal Family's cultural significance lies in its embodiment of cherished values that resonate with the British public. Throughout history, the monarchy has embodied ideals such as duty, service, and tradition. The sovereign is seen as the embodiment of the nation, representing the values and aspirations of the people they serve. Members of the Royal Family often engage in philanthropic work, shining a spotlight on important social issues and championing causes close to their hearts. Their patronages and charitable endeavors contribute to a broader sense of communal responsibility and inspire individuals to get involved and make a difference in their own communities. Beyond their philanthropic endeavors, the Royal Family's commitment to duty and service is seen in their ceremonial roles and public engagements, reinforcing the importance of obligation and dedication to the nation.

In addition to these factors, it is important to highlight the role of public sentiment and the emotional connection that individuals feel toward the Royal Family. The monarchy commands a level of respect and affection that transcends rational reasoning. Countless individuals grow up with tales of royal weddings, coronations, and jubilees, forging a bond that is difficult to explain or quantify. The monarchy serves as a unifying force, fostering a shared sense of identity and belonging amongst citizens from diverse backgrounds. It embodies the concept of a collective identity that binds people together, reinforcing a sense of national pride and unity in an increasingly fragmented society. As custodians of a rich and storied past, the monarchy represents a link to collective heritage and a symbol of continuity. The media's extensive coverage of royal events ensures their global visibility, capturing the imagination of millions and piquing curiosity about the British way of life. Moreover, the Royal Family's embodiment of duty, service, and tradition, as well as their philanthropic endeavors, resonates with the British public's values and inspires active engagement in their communities. Lastly, the emotional connection individuals feel towards the monarchy reinforces a sense of national pride and unity. Together, these factors contribute to the enduring cultural significance of the Royal Family, transcending borders, and captivating the world's attention.

The Monarchy's Political Influence

To fully understand the monarchy's political influence, we need to delve into its historical roots. Monarchies have existed for centuries, with varying systems and levels of power. Throughout history, the monarchy has often been closely intertwined with the political structure of a country, shaping its governance and decision-making processes. This influence can be seen in both constitutional monarchies, where the king or queen's role is mostly ceremonial, and absolute monarchies, where the ruler holds substantial power.

One of the key aspects of the monarchy's political influence is its symbolic significance. The monarchy serves as a unifying force, representing the nation and its values. This can be particularly important in times of crisis or uncertainty, as the monarch provides a sense of stability and continuity. Additionally, the monarchy can act as a neutral figurehead, above the political fray, fostering a sense of national identity and cohesion.

Despite the evolution towards more democratic systems in many countries, where elected officials hold the majority of power, monarchies continue to exert political influence, even if more indirect in nature. In constitutional monarchies, the head of state often plays a crucial role in the legislative process. They may have the power to give royal assent to laws, to grant pardons, and even to dissolve parliament and call for new elections. These powers, although largely ceremonial, can still have a significant impact on the political landscape.

Moreover, the monarchy can contribute to political stability by acting as a check on the government's power. The presence of a monarch can provide a counterbalance to the sometimes turbulent world of politics, ensuring that decisions are made with the long-term interests of the nation in mind. The monarch's status as a symbol of national unity can also help ease tensions between different political factions, as they can rally around a shared respect for the crown.

It is worth noting that the specific extent of the monarchy's political influence varies from country to country. In some constitutional monarchies, such as the United Kingdom or Spain, the monarch's powers are more limited, with the focus on representing the country and its people. In other cases, such as Saudi Arabia or Brunei, the monarchy exercises absolute power and holds significant control over the political process.

In recent years, the role of the monarchy has faced increased scrutiny and debate. This is particularly true when conflicts arise between the monarchy and democratic ideals, such as freedom of speech or equality. Critics argue that an unelected figurehead should not have the power to influence political decisions or hold significant positions of authority. However, proponents of the monarchy argue that its role goes beyond politics, emphasizing its cultural, historical, and unifying significance.

It is important to acknowledge that the monarchy's political influence is not static. Just as political systems evolve, so does the monarchy's role within them. In some countries, there have been efforts to limit the powers of the monarchy, ensuring a more balanced division of authority between the crown and elected officials. This ongoing evolution reflects the desire to create political systems that are accountable, inclusive, and responsive to the needs of the people.

To conclude, the monarchy's political influence is a complex and multi-faceted subject that requires careful examination. By understanding its historical roots, symbolic significance, and evolving role, we can gain a clearer picture of the monarchy's impact on the political landscape. While opinions may vary on the extent and nature of this influence, it is crucial to foster open and informed discussions about the role of the monarchy in modern society. This book aims to provide readers with the necessary knowledge and perspective to engage with these discussions in a thoughtful and informed manner.

Chapter 3: The Lives of Royal Family Members

THE ROYAL CHILDREN: Growing Up in the Spotlight

The Royal Children: Growing Up in the Spotlight

Growing up in the spotlight is a unique experience, but for members of royal families, it is a way of life. The lives of royal children are intricately tied to tradition, duty, and public scrutiny. From birth, they are thrust into a world where every move is analyzed, every gesture meticulously observed. It is a world where they are not only heirs to a throne but also symbols of continuity and stability. The pressure on these young royals is immense, as they navigate their way through childhood and adolescence while fulfilling their ceremonial roles. However, amidst the pomp and circumstance, they also have aspirations, creative pursuits, and the desire for a semblance of normalcy - a challenge that society acknowledges and sympathizes with.

Being in the public eye from such a tender age can have its pros and cons. On one hand, royal children have unparalleled access to education, resources, and an array of experiences that most children can only dream of. Their upbringing is a blend of formality and privilege, with the best tutors, palaces as playgrounds, and a network of mentors to guide them. They are exposed to a vast array of cultures, languages, and global issues, broadening their horizons from an early age. The education of these children is not limited to textbooks and classrooms but extends to first-hand experiences, charity work, and diplomatic engagements.

On the other hand, the constant media attention and the pressure to live up to one's heritage can be overwhelming. The spotlight can cast a long shadow, sometimes robbing them of a carefree childhood or teenage rebellion. The flip side of being the subject of public adoration is that every mistake or blunder is magnified and scrutinized. Their every move is documented, dissected, and often misconstrued. Growing up in celebrity culture, royal children increasingly face the challenges of social media and an insatiable hunger for gossip. Privacy becomes a luxury they seldom enjoy. However, society, recognizing this, often extends empathy to these young royals, understanding the invasive nature of the media and the importance of safeguarding their personal lives.

As they transition from youth to adulthood, royal children eventually find themselves in the interplay between tradition and modernity. Bound by centuries of customs and protocols, they must adapt to the expectations of the contemporary age. They become ambassadors for the monarchy, carrying forward the legacy of their ancestors while simultaneously embracing the changing times. The journey from childhood to adulthood in the royal spotlight is defined by a delicate balance between duty and individualism. Through this process, they carve their unique identities within the constraints of their roles.

The experiences of royal children in the spotlight are not limited to their respective countries. In a world that is increasingly interconnected, these young royals often collaborate on global initiatives, exchange ideas, and build bridges between nations. They utilize their privileged position to champion causes close to their hearts, to promote empathy, and to give a voice to those who are unheard. Their upbringing prepares them for roles as leaders, representatives, and influencers, who can use their platform for the betterment of society. From an early age, these young royals are both symbols and individuals, constantly balancing their duty to their country with their desires for autonomy and personal growth. While navigating the delicate line between tradition and modernity, they embrace their role as global ambassadors and catalysts for change. The public recognizes and appreciates their unique challenges, allowing empathy to guide their perception of these young royals. Ultimately, the lives of royal children are both extraordinary and relatable, reminding us of the universal human longing for purpose, identity, and personal fulfillment.

The Queen: A Lifetime of Service

With a reign spanning over six decades, her dedication and unwavering commitment to duty have made her an enduring symbol of service. This book delves into the life and legacy of the Queen, exploring the key moments, roles, and responsibilities that have shaped her remarkable journey. From her early years as a princess to her role as a symbol of stability and unity, we will uncover the multitude of ways in which Queen Elizabeth II has served her country and the Commonwealth.

Early Years and Education

To truly understand the Queen's lifelong commitment to service, we must first examine her formative years and education. Born on April 21, 1926, Elizabeth Alexandra Mary Windsor was thrust into a life of royalty from the outset. Raised in an environment of privilege, she was nonetheless instilled with a strong sense of duty and responsibility from an early age. Her education, which included private tutors, focused on subjects such as constitutional law, history, and languages, preparing her for the weighty role she would eventually assume. These early experiences laid the foundation for her future as a lifelong servant of the crown.

Ascension and Coronation

Upon the untimely death of her father, King George VI, in 1952, Princess Elizabeth ascended to the throne at the age of 25. This pivotal moment marked the beginning of her lifelong commitment to service. The coronation ceremony that followed in 1953 was a spectacle of pomp and pageantry, with millions of people around the world tuning in to witness the historic event. In her coronation speech, the Queen pledged her dedication to the service of her people, setting the tone for her reign and signaling the enduring commitment that would define her rule.

The Constitutional Role of the Monarch

Beyond the spectacle and ceremonial duties, the Queen's most significant contribution lies in her constitutional role as the head of state. While her powers are largely ceremonial and symbolic, her presence and support are essential for the functioning of the democratic system. The role of the monarch in a constitutional monarchy like Britain is to advise, encourage, and warn, while remaining politically neutral. Through regular meetings with prime ministers, state visits, and the delivery of annual speeches, the Queen provides stability and continuity, ensuring the smooth operation of the government.

Family and Commonwealth

In addition to her role within the United Kingdom, the Queen's commitment to service extends to the 54 nations that make up the Commonwealth. As the symbolic head of this diverse group of countries, she plays an integral role in promoting unity, cooperation, and dialogue among its members. Her numerous state visits and personal engagements have fostered stronger ties and a sense of shared purpose among these nations. Furthermore, the Queen's dedication to her own family has been a source of inspiration and stability, as she balances her public role with her responsibilities as a mother, grandmother, and great-grandmother.

Philanthropy and Patronages

The Queen's commitment to service is also manifested in her extensive philanthropic work and patronages. With a wide range of charitable organizations under her patronage, she has tirelessly supported causes related to education, health, the arts, and the welfare of the armed forces. Her patronages allow her to use her position to amplify the voices of those in need and to champion causes that are close to her heart. Through her charitable efforts, the Queen has demonstrated that service is not just a duty but a reflection of one's values and a means to make a tangible difference in the lives of others.

QUEEN ELIZABETH II'S reign has been a testament to a lifetime of service. From a young princess to the longest-reigning monarch in British history, she has embodied the ideals of duty, dedication, and commitment. Through her constitutional role, her unwavering support for the Commonwealth, and her vast philanthropic endeavors, she has shown that service is not simply an obligation but a true calling. Queen Elizabeth II has become a symbol of stability and unity, navigating the complexities of the modern world with grace, compassion, and an unrelenting desire to make a positive impact. Her legacy will forever be intertwined with the profound impact she has had on the nation and the lives of countless individuals around the globe.

Chapter 4: Behind Closed Doors: The Secrets of the Palace

SCANDALS AND CONTROVERSIES

At its core, the concept of scandal refers to a widespread perception of wrongdoing or impropriety that triggers a sense of shock, outrage, or moral condemnation within a community or society at large. These perceptions are often fueled by the exposure of previously hidden or undisclosed information, such as corruption, sexual misconduct, or other forms of ethical breaches. Scandals can emerge from various spheres, including politics, sports, entertainment, and even academia, and can have far-reaching consequences that extend beyond just the individuals directly involved. They can erode public trust in institutions, undermine social cohesion, and lead to significant political, economic, and legal repercussions. Thus, a thorough investigation of scandals necessitates examining the underlying factors that enable their occurrence and perpetuation.

Controversies, on the other hand, often revolve around contentious issues that elicit divergent opinions, divided loyalties, and heated debates within society. Unlike scandals, controversies may not necessarily involve any wrongdoings, but rather stem from conflicting values, ideologies, or interests. These disputes can emerge from matters related to social justice, human rights, scientific discoveries, religious beliefs, or cultural norms, among others. Controversies have the potential to challenge the status quo, drive social change, and redefine cultural boundaries. However, they can also polarize societies, deepen ideological fault lines, and cause deep divisions that are difficult to reconcile. It is therefore crucial to explore both the causes and consequences of controversies in order to foster constructive dialogues and bridge the gaps between opposing viewpoints.

To comprehend the intricate nature of scandals and controversies, it is essential to analyze their underlying causes and triggers. One key factor often identified in the genesis of scandals is the abuse or misuse of power. Individuals in positions of authority, whether in politics, business, or other fields, may succumb to the temptations that come with their positions, leading to ethical compromises and breaches. Moreover, scandals are often facilitated by systemic failures, such as inadequate oversight, loopholes in regulations, or a culture of corruption that tolerates or even encourages illicit behavior. Uncovering these root causes is crucial in designing and implementing mechanisms that can prevent future scandals and hold accountable those responsible for their occurrence.

Similarly, controversies are frequently ignited by societal changes that challenge established norms, beliefs, or power structures. As societies evolve and become more diverse, contestation of values and clashes of ideologies become more prevalent. Controversies often arise when marginalized groups demand recognition, representation, and inclusivity, clashing with traditional power structures and dominant narratives. By examining the drivers of controversies, scholars, policymakers, and individuals can gain a better understanding of the underlying issues, identify common ground, and foster constructive engagement.

Furthermore, scandals and controversies are not isolated events; they are deeply intertwined with broader social, political, and ethical contexts. A scandal can illuminate underlying systemic problems, uncovering deep-seated corruption, inequality, or injustices within a society. Similarly, controversies can act as a catalyst for social change and challenge prevailing norms, leading to a reassessment of societal priorities and values. Understanding these broader implications helps us to contextualize scandals and controversies, recognizing them as symptoms of more profound societal issues that need to be addressed comprehensively.

To fully grasp the effects of scandals and controversies, it is important to analyze the responses of various stakeholders, including governments, media, individuals, and civil society. Governments play a crucial role in managing and responding to scandals and controversies effectively. Their actions, or lack thereof, can either restore public trust or exacerbate the situation. Media outlets, on the other hand, can shape public perception and narratives surrounding scandals and controversies, influencing public opinion and the outcome of events. Individuals and civil society organizations also have agency in shaping the course of these events through advocacy, public pressure, and collective action. Acknowledging the role and responsibilities of various actors in these incidents is vital to understanding their impact and working towards meaningful resolutions. By examining the causes, triggers, and responses to these events, this book aims to shed light on the multifaceted nature of scandal and controversy and the lessons they offer for society at large. By fostering a better understanding of these phenomena, we can strive for a more transparent, accountable, and inclusive society, one that learns from its mistakes and seeks to prevent and address scandals and controversies proactively.

The Intriguing World of Royal Protocol

The regal figures who inhabit palaces and castles, with their elegant attire, lavish ceremonies, and glamorous lifestyles, seem to exist in a realm unto themselves. While much of this fascination stems from their mythical allure and fairy tale-like existence, it is the intricate web of royal protocol that truly adds depth and significance to their positions. This book aims to explore the captivating world of royal protocol, shedding light on its origins, purpose, and the various rules and customs that govern the lives of the royals. By delving into this fascinating topic, we hope to demystify the world of royalty and allow readers to gain a deeper appreciation for the complexities and nuances that underpin their roles.

The Historical Context of Royal Protocol

To truly understand the nuances of royal protocol, it is essential to appreciate its historical context. The traditions and customs that are associated with royalty have evolved over centuries, shaped by civilizations and socio-political environments. From the ancient Egyptian pharaohs to the medieval monarchs of Europe and the modern British royal family, each era has contributed to the development of royal protocols. These protocols were established to ensure stability, functionality, and the preservation of the monarchy's prestige. By examining the historical roots of royal protocol, we can gain insight into the reasons behind its existence and comprehend its significance in contemporary society.

The Purpose of Royal Protocol

Why is royal protocol important. This question lingers in the minds of many who encounter the intricacies of royal engagements. Not merely a matter of formality, royal protocol serves several purposes. Firstly, it ensures the smooth running of royal events, preventing any unforeseen mishaps that may tarnish the reputation of the monarch. Secondly, protocol provides a sense of structure and hierarchy, both internally among the royals and externally with foreign dignitaries. Furthermore, it has a symbolic function, portraying the monarchy as an institution steeped in tradition, dignity, and cultural heritage. Understanding the role that royal protocol plays in upholding these objectives allows us to appreciate its significance in maintaining the prestige and integrity of royal families.

The Role of Royal Protocol in Diplomacy

While the formality and splendor of royal engagements may appear superficial at first glance, they serve a vital role in diplomatic relations. Royalty acts as a strong bridge between nations, fostering goodwill and representing their respective country's interests. Royal visits, state banquets, and ceremonial occasions create opportunities for heads of state to meet on equal footing, facilitating dialogue and negotiation. Royal protocol ensures that these meetings run smoothly, allowing diplomats to focus on substantive matters. Furthermore, the intricate rules surrounding royal visits and interactions help convey respect and mutual understanding between nations. By exploring the diplomatic aspect of royal protocol, we can gain insight into the behind-the-scenes efforts needed to maintain international relations.

The Impact of Modernity on Royal Protocol

As societies evolve, so too does royal protocol. The advent of modernity and the influence of popular culture have brought about significant changes in how royal families interact with the public and conduct themselves. The rise of social media, for instance, has necessitated a more accessible and relatable approach, allowing the royals to forge closer connections with the public. Traditional protocols have been adapted to accommodate these changes, such as the British royal family's engagement with the public through their social media platforms. This one explores the tension between maintaining the traditions and charm of royal protocol while embracing the demands of a modern world. Understanding these dynamics is essential to comprehending how royal families navigate the complexities of their roles in contemporary society.

Unveiling the Mysteries of Royal Protocol

In this final one, we delve into the intriguing and lesser-known aspects of royal protocol. From the intricate rules surrounding seating arrangements to the symbolism of royal regalia, we aim to shed light on the lesser-understood customs that shape the lives of the royals. We also explore the regional variations in royal protocols, contrasting the pomp and circumstance of European royalty with the more understated traditions of Asian monarchies. By unraveling these mysterious aspects of royal protocol, we hope to provide readers with a comprehensive understanding of this captivating world.

THE WORLD OF ROYAL protocol is a fascinating realm that combines history, tradition, diplomacy, and modernity. While its purpose may initially appear outdated or frivolous, it serves a vital role in upholding the prestige and functionality of monarchies worldwide. Through exploring the historical context, purpose, diplomatic significance, impact of modernity, and lesser-known nuances of royal protocol, this book aims to shed light on this intriguing world. By demystifying royal protocol, we hope to engage readers in a conversation that unravels the complexities of royalty, ultimately fostering a deeper appreciation for the individuals who inhabit this regal domain.

Chapter 5: The Royal Residences

BUCKINGHAM PALACE: The Queen's Official Residence

One cannot help but be captivated by the rich history that permeates the very walls of Buckingham Palace. Its roots can be traced back to the early 18th century when George III purchased the property as a private residence for his queen, Queen Charlotte. Over the years, subsequent monarchs expanded and transformed the palace into the awe-inspiring structure we see today. Architects like John Nash and Sir Aston Webb have left their indelible marks, incorporating various architectural styles and elements, such as Neoclassical and French Renaissance influences, into the palace's design. This amalgamation of architectural styles showcases the evolution of Buckingham Palace over time, making it not only historically significant but also a testament to the changing tastes and preferences of the monarchy.

Beyond its architectural splendor, Buckingham Palace holds an array of cultural artifacts that reflect the royal family's deep-rooted connection with the arts. The palace houses an extensive collection of paintings, sculptures, and decorative arts, amassed over centuries. These priceless treasures offer a glimpse into the cultural heritage of the nation, as well as the personal tastes of the royal family throughout history. Works by renowned artists such as Rembrandt, Van Dyck, and Canaletto adorn the palace walls, exemplifying the royal patronage of the arts and their commitment to preserving the nation's cultural heritage. Exploring these collections allows visitors to appreciate the intersection of art, history, and royal patronage, providing a true insight into the cultural legacy of Buckingham Palace.

Ceremonial occasions are an integral part of the monarchy, and Buckingham Palace serves as the backdrop to some of the most significant events in British royal history. The Changing of the Guard, an iconic ceremony that takes place daily during the summer months, draws crowds of visitors from around the world. This centuries-old tradition, where the new guard relieves the old guard and ceremonially takes over the protection of the palace, is a fine display of precision and military pageantry. The sight of the guards in their resplendent uniforms, accompanied by the stirring beats of the regimental bands, creates a spectacle that embodies the grandeur and tradition of the British monarchy. Attending one of these ceremonies is a memorable experience, allowing visitors to witness living history unfold right before their eyes.

Perhaps the most significant event held at Buckingham Palace is the investiture ceremony. This time-honored tradition, dating back to the days of Queen Victoria, allows individuals to be recognized and honored for their exceptional achievements. In the impressive surroundings of the palace's ballroom, recipients kneel before the monarch, who bestows upon them their well-deserved honors. These honors, symbolized by the touch of a sword or placement of a medal, represent the pinnacle of success in various fields, from arts and sports to science and humanitarian endeavors. Witnessing these investitures is a truly inspiring experience as it celebrates the accomplishments of individuals who have made a substantial contribution to their respective fields and highlights the monarchy's commitment to recognizing excellence.

Beyond its ceremonial and cultural significance, Buckingham Palace is also a functioning royal residence. It houses a vast array of spaces, each serving a specific purpose, be it accommodation for the royal family or hosting official functions. The State Rooms, open to the public during the summer, offer a glimpse into the opulence and grandeur of the palace. These rooms, each impeccably decorated with exquisite furnishings, chandeliers, and priceless artworks, bear witness to the rich heritage of the monarchy. The grand ballroom, with its soaring ceilings and majestic atmosphere, serves as a venue for state banquets, royal balls, and other significant social events. The surrounding gardens, meticulously manicured and impeccably maintained, offer respite from the bustling city, providing a tranquil oasis for the royal family and visitors alike. Its rich history, architectural grandeur, cultural artifacts, ceremonial traditions, and functional role make it an entity that transcends time and resonates with people from all walks of life. Exploring the depths of Buckingham Palace allows us to gain a profound understanding of the monarchy's legacy, the nation's cultural tapestry, and the enduring spirit that ties the palace to the British people. Whether one is an ardent royalist, an art enthusiast, or a history buff, Buckingham Palace remains an indispensable focal point, inviting us to marvel at its magnificence and unravel the secrets held within its hallowed halls.

Windsor Castle: A Royal Retreat

Located in the picturesque town of Windsor, just outside of London, this magnificent fortress has been a royal residence for over nine centuries. With its sprawling grounds, stunning architecture, and captivating history, Windsor Castle offers a unique glimpse into the lives of the British royals throughout the ages. In this book, we will explore the diverse aspects of this remarkable castle, from its origins as a medieval fortress to its current role as a beloved royal retreat.

A Living History

Windsor Castle holds the distinction of being the oldest and largest inhabited castle in the world, giving it an unparalleled status as a living historical site. Built by William the Conqueror in the 11th century, the castle has witnessed countless significant events and royal ceremonies throughout the centuries. From the imposing Round Tower to the lavish State Apartments, each section of the castle reflects a different era and architectural style. As we delve into the castle's rich heritage, we will traverse the iconic St George's Chapel, the beautifully manicured gardens, and the awe-inspiring Great Hall, learning about the individuals and events that have shaped its illustrious past.

Royal Residence and Sanctuary

Windsor Castle has served as a cherished royal residence for generations of British monarchs, providing them with solace, privacy, and a retreat from the demands of public life. Kings and queens have used the stunning rooms and landscapes of the castle as a backdrop for hosting distinguished guests, conducting state affairs, and seeking respite from the world's pressures. We will explore the private apartments of the royal family, their opulent decor, and the exquisite works of art adorning the walls. Furthermore, we will discover the castle's peaceful ambience through its tranquil gardens, picturesque walks, and breathtaking views, all contributing to its role as a sanctuary for royalty.

Majestic Art and Treasures

Windsor Castle houses an extensive collection of art, artifacts, and treasures amassed by successive monarchs over centuries. These treasures offer a unique glimpse into the tastes, preferences, and cultural patronage of the British royal family. From priceless paintings by world-renowned artists to intricate tapestries and historic objets d'art, the castle's collection highlights the key periods and movements in European art history. We will delve into the revered Queen's Gallery, where masterpieces from the Royal Collection are showcased, and explore the castle's renowned Royal Library, which houses a remarkable collection of rare books, manuscripts, and historical documents.

The Castle and the Community

Windsor Castle is not just an architectural marvel; it is also an integral part of the local community and wider society. The castle plays a vital role in sustaining local businesses, supporting the town's cultural activities, and providing employment opportunities. Moreover, it serves as a popular tourist destination, attracting millions of visitors each year, who come to marvel at its grandeur and immerse themselves in its rich history. The castle's management is dedicated to preserving and maintaining this cultural landmark, engaging in numerous conservation, research, and educational initiatives that contribute to the wider understanding and appreciation of this national treasure.

WINDSOR CASTLE STANDS as a true testament to the endurance and grandeur of the British monarchy. Its rich history, architectural beauty, and cultural significance continue to captivate visitors from around the world. This royal retreat, steeped in tradition and its close ties to the monarchy, invites us to walk in the footsteps of kings and queens, immersing ourselves in a world that is both awe-inspiring and intimately human. As we conclude this exploration of Windsor Castle, we are left with a profound appreciation for its role as a symbol of national identity, a sanctuary for the royal family, and a living testament to the enduring legacy of the British monarchy.

Chapter 6: The Royal Finances

THE COST OF MAINTAINING the Monarchy

However, in today's modern societies, questions have been raised regarding the necessity and cost-effectiveness of maintaining a monarchy. While some argue that the monarchy brings stability, tradition, and national identity, others question the financial burden it places on taxpayers. In this discussion, we will delve into the various facets of the cost of maintaining a monarchy, shedding light on its economic implications, avenues for cost reduction, and the potential benefits of retaining such an institution.

The Financial Reality:

Critics of the monarchical system often point to the inherent costliness of sustaining a royal family. These expenses primarily include the maintenance of palaces, transportation, security, and official engagements. In countries like the United Kingdom, the Royal Family's funding primarily comes from the Sovereign Grant, which is a portion of the Crown Estate's annual profits allocated to the monarchy. For the fiscal year 2020-2021, the Sovereign Grant stood at £85.9 million (approximately $114.3 million). This figure is intended to cover official duties and the maintenance of the royal residences. However, it is worth noting that while the direct monarchical expenses are significant, they often constitute a meager percentage of a nation's overall budget.

Preserving Tradition and National Identity:

Proponents of maintaining a monarchy argue that the institution embodies centuries-old traditions, acting as a cultural symbol and preserving national identity. A monarchy's continuity ensures that historical and cultural heritage is not lost to the passage of time. This sense of continuity fosters a collective identity and pride among citizens, allowing them to connect with their roots and shared history. The pomp and ceremony associated with royal events also draw international tourists, generating revenue for the local economy and supporting various ancillary businesses.

Comparing Constitutional Monarchies and Republics:

It is essential to consider the alternatives to constitutional monarchies and weigh their potential costs against those of maintaining a monarchy. Republics, characterized by a president as head of state, often incur expenses related to presidential elections, campaigning, and maintaining presidential estates. Additionally, former presidents may receive lifelong pensions, security protection, and continued staff support. While these costs may vary across different countries, the comparisons underline that the systems of governance have inherent costs, regardless of the specific framework chosen.

Beneficial Economic Impacts:

Contrary to popular belief, the monarchy can have positive economic impacts on a nation. The tourism sector, in particular, benefits greatly from royal heritage, attracting visitors who wish to witness iconic ceremonies, explore historical palaces, or even catch a glimpse of a monarch. According to estimates by VisitBritain, royal tourism contributed £2.7 billion (approximately $3.6 billion) to the UK economy in 2019. These funds not only support local businesses surrounding key royal sites but also generate tax revenue. Additionally, royal weddings and other high-profile events draw worldwide attention, providing a platform to promote national industries, culture, and tourism.

Pruning the Expenses:

Recognizing the concerns related to the cost of maintaining the monarchy, several steps have been taken in recent years to reduce expenses and increase transparency. These include the Estate Rationalization Program, which involves reviewing the Crown Estate's operational costs and optimizing the utilization of properties. Similarly, the Royal Household has implemented measures to reduce energy consumption and has taken on commercial ventures, such as leasing unused properties, to generate supplementary income. Additionally, calls for stricter oversight and increased accountability have led to greater scrutiny and public reporting of royal finances.

THE COST OF MAINTAINING a monarchy continues to be a subject of debate in modern society. While some view the expenses as excessive, it is essential to consider the broader implications and benefits that come with preserving traditions, culture, and national identity. The monarchy's impact on tourism, local economies, and international relations cannot be overlooked. However, efforts to increase fiscal prudence and transparency must be an ongoing priority. Ultimately, societies must weigh the cost against the intangible benefits that the monarchy brings and carefully consider the alternatives and their respective costs before making any decisions regarding the future of their governance structures.

The Wealth of the Royal Family

To begin with, it is crucial to understand that the wealth of royal families is primarily derived from inherited assets and investments, rather than personal earnings or salaries. In many cases, these assets have been acquired and accumulated over several generations, making it difficult to determine the exact value of their wealth. Moreover, royal families often have diverse portfolios, including real estate, art collections, and holdings in businesses and corporations, which further complicates any accurate evaluation of their total worth.

One of the common misconceptions is that royal families receive large sums of money from taxpayers. While it is true that some monarchies receive public funds to support their official duties and maintain their residences, these funds are typically allocated through a system of grants approved by the government. The purpose of these grants is to cover the costs of royal duties, such as state visits, ceremonial events, and palace maintenance.

In some countries, such as the United Kingdom, the monarchy has undergone significant reforms in recent years to make it more transparent and accountable. The Sovereign Grant, introduced in 2011, replaced the traditional Civil List and provides a fixed annual amount to support the British royal family. This grant is drawn from the revenue generated by the Crown Estate, a vast property portfolio owned by the monarchy but managed independently. The Crown Estate includes prime properties in central London, commercial parks, and offshore wind farms, among other assets. The revenue generated from these properties is used to fund the Sovereign Grant, with any surplus being returned to the treasury.

It is worth noting that the Sovereign Grant covers only official expenses. Personal expenses, such as private travel, are often paid for by the royal family themselves or through other sources, such as the Duchy of Lancaster or the Duchy of Cornwall, which are private estates held by the British monarch and the heir apparent, respectively. These estates also generate income that contributes to the overall wealth of the royal family.

Similarly, other royal families around the world have different financial arrangements. Some may receive funds directly from the government, while others may rely on private income from sources such as investments or personal estates. It is essential to consider the cultural and historical context of each monarchy to understand their specific financial situation.

Beyond public funding, there are also significant economic contributions that royal families make to their countries. For instance, the British royal family is estimated to generate billions of pounds in tourism revenue each year, as millions of tourists visit historical sites and landmarks associated with the monarchy. The same can be said for other countries that have a rich royal heritage, attracting visitors who want to learn about their history and traditions.

It is also worth highlighting that the wealth of royal families goes beyond monetary value. They often have a rich cultural and historical legacy that contributes to the preservation of national heritage. Through their patronage of the arts, support for charitable causes, and promotion of cultural diplomacy, royal families play a crucial role in promoting and preserving the arts, history, and culture of their respective countries. While they do enjoy significant assets and investments, it is important to have a nuanced understanding of their financial arrangements and contributions. By examining the diverse sources of their wealth, including inherited assets, investment portfolios, and public and private funding arrangements, we can gain a more comprehensive understanding of the wealth of the royal family. Additionally, by considering the economic and cultural contributions they make to their countries, we can appreciate the broader impact of their wealth beyond its monetary value.

Chapter 7: The Influence of the Monarchy on British Culture

ROYAL WEDDINGS: A NATIONAL Celebration

Whether it is the grandeur, the tradition, or the love story that captures our hearts, these events hold a unique place in our collective consciousness. This book aims to dive deeper into the significance and the magic that surrounds these joyous occasions. From historical context to the modern-day extravaganza, we will explore the traditions, the cultural impact, and the lasting legacies of royal weddings.

The History of Royal Weddings

To truly appreciate royal weddings as a national celebration, it is essential to delve into their historical roots. Royal unions have been a part of human civilization for centuries, cementing alliances, strengthening political ties, or blending different cultures. The significance of these events in transforming not only the lives of the royals themselves but also the course of nations cannot be overstated. From the famed wedding of Queen Victoria to Prince Albert, which initiated the trend of white wedding gowns, to the more recent nuptials of Prince William and Kate Middleton that enthralled the world, these moments have left an indelible mark in history.

Tradition, Ritual, and Pageantry

One of the undeniable draws of royal weddings is the rich tapestry of tradition, ritual, and pageantry they bring to the forefront. From the majestic processions that take place in the streets to the ceremonial exchange of vows within the hallowed halls of grand cathedrals, every aspect of a royal wedding is curated to reflect centuries-old customs. The book will explore the symbolism behind various elements of the ceremony, from the meaning of the bridal bouquet to the significance of the exchanging of rings. Understanding these traditions adds a layer of appreciation for the intricate planning and attention to detail that goes into making these events truly magical.

The Cultural Impact

Royal weddings have the remarkable ability to captivate the public's imagination and transcend geographic boundaries. They become cultural touchstones, inspiring fashion trends, sparking conversations, and eliciting a sense of national pride. By examining the cultural impact of royal weddings, we can discern how these celebrations shape popular imagination, inject new life into local economies through tourism and memorabilia, and even influence the choice of baby names or wedding themes for years to come. From Princess Diana's iconic dress to Meghan Markle's choice to honor her African-American heritage, royal weddings have the power to foster inclusivity and reflect the diversity of the modern world.

Modern-Day Extravaganza

In recent times, royal weddings have evolved into spectacular displays of opulence and grandeur, showcasing the best of contemporary design, technology, and entertainment. With the world as their audience, royal couples incorporate elements that resonate with the present time, creating a sense of relevance and excitement. From the star-studded guest lists to the breathtaking venues, nothing is left to chance when it comes to creating these immersive experiences. This one will explore how these modern-day weddings have adapted to reflect the changing times while still retaining the timeless qualities that make them so beloved.

The Lasting Legacy

Beyond the pomp and glamour, royal weddings often leave a lasting legacy that extends far beyond the individual couple's happily ever after. From the philanthropic causes championed by royal newlyweds to the impact on public perceptions of the monarchy, these celebrations have long-term effects on society. By examining the charitable initiatives launched in connection with royal weddings, we can witness the enduring societal impact that these events have. Additionally, we will explore how royal weddings contribute to the popularity and support for the monarchy, helping to maintain its relevance in the modern world.

ROYAL WEDDINGS HOLD an esteemed place in our hearts as a national celebration. From their historical significance to the cultural impact and the modern-day extravaganza they embody, these joyous occasions leave an indelible mark on society. Through understanding the traditions, rituals, and pageantry associated with royal weddings, we gain a deeper appreciation for the meticulous planning and attention to detail involved. Additionally, we witness the transformative power of these events, both in shaping popular culture and fostering a sense of national pride. It is through exploring the lasting legacies that we truly realize the impact of these celebrations on society. Ultimately, royal weddings are more than just fairy tales; they are an integral part of our cultural fabric.

The Monarchy and the Media

In many ways, the monarchy and the media have a symbiotic relationship. The media acts as a platform through which the monarchy communicates with the public, while the monarchy offers the media exclusive access and important stories. The media is fascinated by the lives of royalty, and the public has an insatiable appetite for news and information about their favorite royals. This mutual interest ensures that the monarchy remains in the public eye, allowing it to wield influence and play a significant role in the governance of a nation.

However, with the advancements in technology and the rise of social media, the relationship between the monarchy and the media has become more complex. The media landscape has changed dramatically, with traditional newspapers and television networks no longer holding a monopoly on news dissemination. Individuals are now able to access news instantaneously through various online platforms, placing the monarchy under constant scrutiny.

The monarchs and members of the royal family are more accessible than ever before, thanks to the advent of social media. Platforms such as Instagram and Twitter have given them the ability to connect directly with the public, bypassing traditional media channels. This newfound accessibility has both advantages and disadvantages. On one hand, it allows the monarchy to control their own narrative and present themselves in a more relatable and approachable manner. On the other hand, it exposes them to increased scrutiny and the potential for negative coverage.

The media has a duty to report accurately and responsibly on the activities of the monarchy. However, sensationalism and scandal often dominate the headlines, leading to a distorted image of the royal family. Tabloid journalism, in particular, tends to focus on the personal lives of the monarchs and their family members, often disregarding their official duties and contributions to society. This tabloid culture can be damaging to the reputation of the monarchy and may create a false perception of their role and significance.

Moreover, the media's coverage of the monarchy can sometimes be influenced by political agendas. The monarchy is often seen as a symbol of national unity and continuity, and politicians may seek to gain favor with the public by aligning themselves with the monarchy or using them for political purposes. This can lead to biased reporting and the manipulation of public opinion.

Despite these challenges, the monarchy remains one of the most enduring and respected institutions in many countries. It serves as a unifying force, representing national identity and heritage. The media, with its wide reach and influence, plays a crucial role in shaping public perception of the monarchy. It is important for the media to strike a balance between reporting on the personal lives of the royals and highlighting their contributions to society. The media serves as a powerful tool through which the monarchy communicates with the public, while the monarchy offers the media exclusive access and important stories. However, the media's coverage of the monarchy can sometimes be sensationalistic, biased, or influenced by political agendas. It is crucial for the media to report accurately and responsibly on the activities of the monarchy, allowing the public to form informed opinions and appreciate the true significance of this institution.

Chapter 8: The Future of the Royal Family

SUCCESSION AND THE Line of the Throne

The transfer of power from one ruler to the next has shaped history and influenced the trajectory of nations. Understanding the dynamics of succession and the intricacies of the line of the throne is essential for comprehending the political landscape of a monarchy. This one explores the various factors that determine succession, the challenges it poses, and the significance of the line of the throne in maintaining stability and continuity within a royal institution.

Factors Influencing Succession:

Succession in a monarchy can be influenced by a variety of factors, including primogeniture, gender, and geography. Primogeniture, the principle of passing the crown to the eldest child, is a common form of succession. This approach ensures a smooth transition of power and maintains the order of succession within a dynasty. However, there have been instances where other factors, such as the monarch's personal choice or a council decision, have overridden primogeniture.

Gender also plays a significant role in determining succession. Many monarchies historically favored male heirs over female ones, but this paradigm has been challenged in recent years. Several countries, including Sweden and Belgium, have implemented gender-neutral succession laws, allowing equal inheritance rights to both male and female heirs. This shift towards gender equality in succession reflects a growing recognition of the importance of fairness and inclusivity within a royal institution.

Geography can also impact succession. Different regions may have distinctive traditions and customs regarding the line of succession. In some cases, these regional variations have led to conflicts between branches of a royal family. Careful management of these regional differences is crucial to maintaining unity and stability within a monarchy.

Challenges to Succession:

Succession is not without challenges, and the line of the throne can be fraught with complexities. One significant challenge is the potential for power struggles within a dynasty. Competing factions may emerge, each advocating for their preferred candidate to assume the throne. These internal rivalries can lead to divisions within the royal family and create instability within the monarchy.

Another challenge lies in securing a clear line of succession. This is particularly relevant when there are multiple potential heirs or when determining the rightful successor becomes a matter of contention. Legal frameworks, such as the establishment of succession laws or the creation of royal councils, are often employed to mitigate these challenges and ensure a smooth transition of power.

The Significance of the Line of the Throne:

The line of the throne plays a crucial role in maintaining stability and continuity within a royal institution. It represents a link to the past, embodying the traditions, values, and heritage of a monarch and their dynasty. The line of the throne also carries immense symbolic weight, signifying a connection between the ruler and the people they govern.

For the monarchy to retain legitimacy and public support, continuity is paramount. The line of succession ensures that there is always a clear successor to assume the throne, preventing power vacuums and the potential for political turmoil. By upholding the line of the throne, a monarchy can foster a sense of security and continuity, providing a stable environment for the nation to thrive.

In addition to stability, the line of the throne serves as a unifying force. It allows the public to rally around a common figure, someone who embodies the nation's ideals and values. The line of the throne provides a sense of national identity and pride, strengthening the bond between the monarchy and its subjects.

SUCCESSION AND THE line of the throne are vital components of any monarchy. Understanding the factors that influence succession, the challenges it poses, and the significance of the line of the throne is essential for comprehending the dynamics of royal institutions. By carefully managing succession and upholding the line of the throne, monarchies can ensure stability, continuity, and the public's ongoing support for generations to come.

The Monarchy in a Changing World

In this book, we will delve into several aspects of the monarchy, including its historical significance, the evolving roles of monarchs, and its place in society amidst a rapidly changing global landscape. By examining different perspectives and providing a comprehensive analysis, we aim to shed light on one of the oldest and most enduring institutions in the world.

The Historical Significance of Monarchy

Monarchy, as a form of governance, has a deep-rooted historical significance that spans across continents and cultures. By examining the origins of monarchy in various societies, we can appreciate how it shaped the political landscape throughout history. From ancient Egypt to medieval Europe and modern constitutional monarchies, the institution has evolved to accommodate diverse societal needs and values. Understanding this historical backdrop allows us to contextualize the role of monarchy in today's world.

The Evolving Role of Monarchs

Over the centuries, the role of monarchs has undergone significant transformations. Once seen as absolute rulers, monarchs have progressively assumed more ceremonial and symbolic roles, with political power often yielding to constitutional frameworks. Examining these shifts helps us grasp the reasons behind the survival and relevance of monarchies in many nations despite changing political dynamics. We will explore case studies of modern monarchies and the ways in which monarchs contribute to their respective societies through diplomacy, charity work, and being national figureheads.

Monarchy and Democracy

In an interconnected and democratizing world, the relationship between monarchy and democracy requires careful examination. Some argue that monarchies are inherently undemocratic, whereas others contend that these institutions can provide stability and a sense of national identity even within democratic systems. By analyzing constitutional monarchies, such as those in the United Kingdom, Spain, and Japan, we can evaluate the compatibility between monarchy and democratic principles. We will also address the potential challenges and benefits associated with combining these seemingly contrasting systems.

The Monarchy's Role in Society

Monarchs have historically played an integral role in society by acting as unifying figures and embodying national symbolism. In this one, we will explore the impact of the monarchy on social cohesion and cultural identity. By examining public opinion, celebrations, and monarchial influence on tourism and the economy, we can gauge the extent to which the monarchy resonates with citizens and its tangible and intangible effects on society at large.

The Monarchy in a Globalized World

As our world becomes more interconnected and globalized, the monarchy faces new challenges and opportunities. With the advent of social media and increased international collaboration, monarchs now hold a unique position in shaping public opinion and diplomacy. We will explore the ways in which modern monarchies have adapted to this changing landscape and how they contribute to international relations, serving as ambassadors of their nations and forging diplomatic ties across borders. By examining its history, evolution, relationship with democracy, societal impact, and role in a globalized context, we can better understand the multifaceted nature of monarchies. Though subject to ongoing debates, the monarchy persists as a symbol of continuity, tradition, and, in some cases, a cornerstone of national identity. Through this exploration, we hope to foster a deeper appreciation for this enduring institution and its place in our ever-transforming world.

Chapter 9: Royal Tradition and Ceremony

THE STATE OPENING OF Parliament

To understand the State Opening of Parliament, we must first examine its historical roots. Dating back to the 16th century, this tradition emerged as a way for monarchs to formally open a new parliamentary session, seeking consent for proposed legislation. Over time, this ceremony evolved into a powerful symbol of the relationship between the crown and parliament, highlighting the constitutional role each plays in the governance of the nation. Today, the State Opening of Parliament serves as a vivid reminder of the foundations upon which modern British democracy was built.

At the heart of this occasion is the reigning monarch, who plays a central role in the State Opening of Parliament. Dressed in regal attire, the sovereign travels from Buckingham Palace to the Palace of Westminster in a lavish procession, accompanied by an impressive display of royal guards and horse-drawn carriages. This extraordinary spectacle is not just a demonstration of pageantry but also a vivid representation of the monarch's constitutional duty to open the new parliamentary session. In recent years, Queen Elizabeth II has fulfilled this role with grace and dignity, further cementing the importance of this tradition in the eyes of the nation.

Accompanying the monarch is the Prince of Wales, a role undertaken by the heir to the throne. This position illustrates the continuity and stability of the monarchy, emphasizing the seamless transfer of power that is central to the British constitutional system. The presence of the Prince of Wales serves as a reminder that the State Opening of Parliament is not solely an event of grandeur and spectacle, but also an occasion of profound symbolism and constitutional significance. It epitomizes the legacy of the British monarchy, which has adapted and thrived over the centuries.

The State Opening of Parliament is also attended by many figures from the realm of politics. Members of both the House of Lords and the House of Commons come together to witness this historic event, signifying their allegiance to the Crown and their commitment to serving the nation. The Prime Minister, the Cabinet, and the Leader of the Opposition are among the prominent individuals in attendance, further highlighting the importance of parliamentary democracy in the United Kingdom. This gathering of politicians underscores the interconnectedness between the monarchy, government, and the legislature, showcasing the delicate balance between the institutions that shape the nation's governance.

One of the most symbolic aspects of the State Opening of Parliament is the reading of the Queen's Speech. This speech, written by the government but delivered by Her Majesty, outlines the legislative agenda for the coming session, presenting the policies and priorities of the ruling party. The Queen's Speech serves as a blueprint for the government's plans, allowing for parliamentary debate and scrutiny. This crucial element of the State Opening of Parliament reinforces the democratic principles upon which the country is founded, showcasing the power of dialogue and deliberation in shaping the nation's future.

In addition to the pageantry and symbolic gestures, the State Opening of Parliament is also a practical affair. Security measures are paramount, with the Palace of Westminster undergoing rigorous checks in preparation for the event. The ceremony itself requires meticulous planning, involving the coordination of various staff members, from those responsible for the logistics to the individuals who handle the state regalia. These practical considerations ensure that this grand pageant can take place smoothly and securely, allowing the nation to witness an occasion that seamlessly weaves together history, tradition, and modern governance.

The State Opening of Parliament is a truly remarkable event that captivates the imagination of individuals both in the United Kingdom and around the world. Its historical significance, the role of the monarch, the presence of political figures, and the reading of the Queen's Speech all contribute to its allure. This occasion, steeped in centuries of tradition, is a testament to the strength and resilience of British democracy. By examining the State Opening of Parliament in detail, this book aims to provide readers with an in-depth understanding of the history, symbolism, and significance behind this extraordinary spectacle. Whether one is a constitutional enthusiast, history buff, or simply curious about the inner workings of the British political system, the State Opening of Parliament is a topic that offers endless fascination and insight into the foundations of modern governance.

Trooping the Colour: A Royal Celebration

In the heart of London, amidst the grandeur of Buckingham Palace and the lush green surroundings of St. James's Park, trooping the colour stands as a time-honored tradition that captures the essence of British heritage and pageantry. This awe-inspiring event, steeped in history and unparalleled in its grandeur, is a ceremonial spectacle that commemorates the official birthday of the reigning monarch. Trooping the Colour is a celebration that not only unites the nation but also captivates the imagination of spectators from around the world, with its exquisite display of military precision, vibrant colors, and majestic splendor.

The origins of Trooping the Colour can be traced back to the 17th century when English or Welsh regiments were required by their sovereign to parade in front of their units, displaying their regimental colors, or flags, as a statement of loyalty and recognition. Over time, this military tradition evolved, merging with the reigning monarch's birthday celebrations, further solidifying the bond between the crown and the armed forces. Today, Trooping the Colour has become synonymous with the official birthday celebrations of the reigning monarch, providing a platform for the public to witness the unity, discipline, and splendor that define the British Armed Forces.

The highlight of Trooping the Colour is the impressive and meticulously choreographed Trooping of the Colour ceremony itself. The ceremony begins with the arrival of the Queen's Guard, resplendent in their red tunics and bearskin caps, who are responsible for guarding the royal palaces. As the time draws near for the monarch's arrival, anticipation hangs in the air, and the crowd eagerly awaits the enthralling moment.

As the clock strikes 11 am, the Queen or the reigning monarch arrives in a majestic horse-drawn carriage, accompanied by the resounding cheers and applause of the gathered crowd. This moment is not merely a display of regal opulence, but a symbolic act of unity and solidarity, as the monarch's presence brings together the nation to celebrate a shared heritage and sense of belonging.

The ceremony unfurls with military precision, as the regiments and military bands parade in front of the sovereign. The Queen takes her position on the imposing Horse Guards Parade ground, with the flag (or colour) being trooped, or carried, in front of her. This trooping of the colour refers to the ceremonial movement during which the regimental flag is paraded meticulously in front of the troops, ensuring the flag is visible to all. It is a symbol of the devotion and loyalty of the soldiers to their monarch and country.

Accompanied by the glorious sound of military bands, including the world-renowned Household Division bands and Corps of Drums, the ceremony exudes a rhythm and grandeur that is both captivating and uplifting. The synchronized movements of the troops, the precision of their drills, and the immaculate handling of their weapons form a breathtaking spectacle that leaves an indelible imprint on the hearts of those fortunate enough to witness it.

The vibrant colors boldly displayed in the uniforms of the regiments and the flags carried during the ceremony evoke a sense of pride and history. The Queen's Guard, the Household Cavalry, and various regiments of the British Army, resplendent in their scarlet tunics, bearskin caps, and intricately designed uniforms, add to the majesty of the occasion. The sight of the soldiers marching in perfect unison, to the beat of accompanying drums, is a testament to the unwavering dedication and professionalism of the British Armed Forces.

The significance of Trooping the Colour extends far beyond its visual spectacle. It is an event that symbolizes the common values and sense of duty shared by the monarchy, the military, and the people of Britain. It is a moment that unites the diverse tapestry of this nation, transcending differences and reminding us of our shared identity.

Trooping the Colour is not merely a celebration for the royal family, but a cherished tradition that stirs emotions and provides an opportunity for people from all walks of life to come together in celebration. The event is attended by thousands of Londoners and tourists, who flock to the streets and parks surrounding Buckingham Palace, ready to witness this iconic display of British heritage and tradition.

In recent years, the popularity and global reach of Trooping the Colour have grown exponentially. Thanks to live television broadcasts and digital media, people from all corners of the globe can experience the magic of this royal celebration. The captivating pomp and ceremony, the visually striking regalia, and the indomitable spirit of the British people come together to create an event that not only showcases British culture but also serves as a testament to the enduring allure of royalty and tradition.

Trooping the Colour stands as a poignant reminder of the steadfastness of the monarchy, the dedication of the armed forces, and the unity of the British people. It is a glorious celebration that transcends time and place, connecting us to the ancient traditions of our past while symbolizing the strength and vibrancy of our present. This pageant of regal splendor continues to captivate hearts and minds, inspiring a sense of pride and celebration that is distinctly British.

Chapter 10: Public Perception of the Royal Family

THE MONARCHY'S POPULARITY

One of the main reasons for the popularity of the monarchy is its historical significance. Monarchies have existed for centuries, and many nations have deep-rooted traditions and customs associated with their monarchy. The monarchy represents a connection to the past, to the time when kings and queens ruled with absolute power. This deep historical connection creates a sense of pride and loyalty among the citizens, as it reminds them of their country's rich heritage and cultural identity.

Furthermore, the monarchy often serves as a unifying force within a nation. As a symbolic figurehead, the monarch represents the unity and stability of the country. In times of national crisis or celebration, the monarch acts as a focal point for the citizens to rally around. The royal family, with its ceremonial duties and public engagements, fosters a sense of collective identity and shared values, promoting a sense of belonging among the people. This feeling of togetherness strengthens the popularity and support for the monarchy.

Another crucial aspect of the monarchy's popularity lies in the personal qualities and actions of the monarch. The charisma, grace, and dignified demeanor of a monarch can significantly influence public opinion. A monarch who embodies these qualities and engages with the public in a genuine and warm manner can easily win the hearts of the people. The media plays a significant role in shaping the public's perception of the royal family, and positive coverage of their activities and engagements can enhance their popularity. On the other hand, any negative behavior or scandals involving the royal family can tarnish the monarchy's reputation and lead to a decline in popularity.

Furthermore, the monarchy's popularity often extends beyond national borders. In many countries, the monarchy is viewed as a symbol of stability and tradition. Tourists from around the world are often drawn to countries with monarchies, eager to witness the pomp and pageantry associated with royal ceremonies and events. This international interest not only brings economic benefits to the country but also generates positive publicity and global recognition, further augmenting the popularity of the monarchy.

However, it is important to note that the popularity of the monarchy is not without its critics. In modern times, as societies become increasingly democratic and meritocratic, some view the monarchy as an outdated and undemocratic institution. The idea of a hereditary position of power can be seen as contrary to the principles of equality and fairness. Additionally, the royal family's lavish lifestyle and privileged position can be perceived as disconnected from the realities of everyday life experienced by the general population. These criticisms can create challenges for the monarchy in maintaining its popularity and relevance in today's society. It is rooted in tradition, history, and a sense of national identity, but can also be influenced by the personal qualities and actions of the monarch, as well as changing societal values. The monarchy serves as a unifying force within a nation and often enjoys international recognition. However, it is not immune to criticism, as some question its compatibility with democratic ideals.

Chapter 11: The Royal Family and Global Diplomacy

ROYAL VISITS AND STATE Banquets

To fully appreciate the importance of royal visits and state banquets, it is necessary to understand their historical roots. The tradition of hosting visiting dignitaries in a regal manner dates back to medieval times when kings and queens ceremoniously welcomed foreign sovereigns to their courts. These encounters were not merely social gatherings, but rather opportunities for diplomacy and showcasing the power and prestige of the hosting nation. Over time, the nature of these visits transformed from displaying wealth and strength to promoting diplomatic alliances and fostering international goodwill.

One of the most iconic features of a royal visit is the state banquet – an elaborate feast held in honor of the visiting monarch or head of state. State banquets are meticulously planned affairs that serve as both a display of culinary excellence and an expression of cultural diplomacy. The menu often represents a fusion of national cuisines, meticulously tailored to the guest's preferences or dietary requirements. These banquets provide an opportunity for the hosting nation to showcase its culinary prowess and promote its rich gastronomic heritage to an international audience.

Aside from the gastronomic splendor, state banquets are also known for their ceremonial aspects. The event is usually held in a grand ballroom or banquet hall within a royal palace or government building, adorned with opulent decorations and elegant table settings. The seating plan follows a strict protocol, designed to reflect the diplomatic hierarchy and honor the guest of honor appropriately. It is not uncommon for these banquets to be accompanied by live music, performed by renowned orchestras or choirs, adding yet another layer of sophistication to the overall experience.

While the aesthetic grandeur plays a crucial role in royal visits and state banquets, it is important to remember that these events are not limited to pomp and circumstance; they are platforms for diplomacy. Discussions held during the visit often revolve around key issues of mutual interest, fostering dialogue and understanding between nations. These high-level meetings are aimed at strengthening bilateral relations, promoting trade and investment, and addressing global challenges collectively. State banquets, in this context, serve as an informal setting where leaders can engage in more relaxed and friendly conversations, building personal rapport and establishing trust.

The significance of royal visits and state banquets in contemporary diplomacy cannot be overstated. While the world has become increasingly interconnected through technological advancements, these formal occasions provide a unique opportunity for face-to-face engagement between leaders. In an era dominated by virtual interactions, the personal touch and cultural exchanges facilitated by such visits contribute to fostering diplomatic understanding and cooperation. Moreover, the media attention surrounding these events ensures that their messages reach a global audience, amplifying their impact and allowing for fruitful diplomacy on a broader scale. Their historical significance, ceremonial aspects, and contemporary relevance all contribute to their effectiveness as diplomatic tools. These events serve as platforms for showcasing cultural heritage, promoting bilateral relations, and facilitating meaningful dialogue between nations. In an ever-changing world, the tradition of royal visits and state banquets continues to evolve, adapting to contemporary diplomatic needs while preserving their essence as symbols of diplomatic elegance and international cooperation.

The Monarchy's Role in International Relations

Monarchies, with their unique position as both heads of state and symbols of national identity, play a significant role in shaping a country's foreign policy and diplomatic efforts. This one aims to shed light on the various aspects of the monarchy's involvement in international relations, exploring both historical perspectives and modern examples. While focusing on the positive contributions and potential limitations of monarchies, we must recognize that the role of monarchy varies greatly across different countries and their particular political systems.

Historical Context:

Throughout history, monarchy has often been the primary representative of a nation in international affairs. Kings and queens possessed considerable power and authority, allowing them to establish diplomatic relations, negotiate treaties, and engage in various forms of diplomacy. Monarchies played a pivotal role in maintaining stability within their realms and projecting their nations' interests abroad. For instance, during the Renaissance, monarchs like King Francis I of France and Queen Elizabeth I of England played significant roles in international politics, forming alliances and exerting their influence to maintain their kingdoms' security and enhance their national prestige.

Modern Role:

As contemporary political systems have evolved, so too has the role of monarchy in international relations. In constitutional monarchies, where the monarch's powers are limited and largely symbolic, the responsibility for foreign policy lies with the elected government. However, the monarchy still serves as an essential representative figurehead, symbolizing the unity and continuity of the nation. In many cases, the monarchy acts as a neutral and non-partisan voice, fostering international goodwill and serving as a unifying force.

In countries like the United Kingdom and the Netherlands, where constitutional monarchies exist, the monarch's role in international relations is often ceremonial. They receive foreign dignitaries, attend state visits, and engage in cultural diplomacy to promote their countries abroad. These activities not only enhance bilateral relations but also contribute to fostering broader international understanding.

Furthermore, monarchs can act as influential advocates for global issues, leveraging their positions to raise awareness and rally support for humanitarian, environmental, and social causes. Their involvement in various charitable initiatives provides a powerful platform to address pressing international challenges. For instance, Queen Rania of Jordan has been a prominent advocate for education and women's rights, using her position to advance these causes internationally.

Soft Power Projection:

Monarchies often possess a unique soft power, contributing to their countries' international standing. Their long-standing history, traditions, and cultural heritage make them objects of fascination and curiosity for people around the world. This soft power can be utilized to strengthen diplomatic ties, attract foreign investment, and promote tourism and cultural exchanges. The British royal family, for instance, attracts millions of tourists each year, boosting the country's economy through royal events, such as weddings or jubilees.

Additionally, the monarchy can serve as a source of stability in the ever-changing world of international relations. In times of political instability or transition, the presence of a monarchy can provide a sense of continuity, anchoring the country and providing reassurance to foreign actors in their interactions. This stability is particularly important for countries with emerging democracies or nations recovering from conflicts.

Potential Limitations:

However, it is also important to acknowledge the potential limitations of monarchies in international relations. The hereditary nature of monarchy raises concerns about the concentration of power and the lack of accountability. In democratic societies, citizens expect their leaders to be accountable to them through electoral processes, which is not applicable to monarchies. Critics argue that the lack of direct public accountability may hinder the transparency and responsiveness of the monarchy's actions in international affairs.

Moreover, the monarchy's involvement in foreign policy must align with national interests and the elected government's agenda. At times, conflicts or differences of opinion may arise between the monarch and the government, creating potential challenges in maintaining a consistent and coherent foreign policy approach. However, in well-established constitutional monarchies, the monarch's role is largely ceremonial and non-political, limiting the potential for such conflicts. While their responsibilities and powers may vary across different countries, monarchies play a vital role in upholding national identity, projecting soft power, and enhancing diplomatic ties. The symbolism and cultural significance associated with the monarchy often provide a source of pride, stability, and continuity for the nation. However, it is crucial to strike a balance between the potential benefits of monarchies and the need for democratic accountability and responsiveness in foreign policy decision-making. By understanding and appreciating the complexities of the monarchy's role, we can engage in informed discussions and assessments of their significance in the ever-changing world of international relations.

45

Chapter 12: The Monarchy and Social Issues

THE ROYAL FAMILY'S Charitable Work

This one delves into the philanthropic endeavors of the Royal Family, discussing the scope and significance of their charitable work. We will explore the various causes they champion, the organisations they support, and the long-lasting effects of their efforts, highlighting the crucial role they play in raising awareness and funds for those in need.

The Scope and Variety of Charitable Causes:

The Royal Family's charitable work spans a broad spectrum of areas, ranging from social issues to environmental conservation. It is evident that they possess a genuine concern for the welfare of communities both within the United Kingdom and around the world. Their commitment to addressing social challenges is evident in their endeavors to combat poverty, homelessness, mental health issues, and the inclusion of marginalized groups. Moreover, the Royal Family recognizes the importance of protecting the environment, supporting initiatives aimed at preserving natural resources, biodiversity, and tackling climate change. By backing these causes, they cement their role as catalysts for positive change.

Organizations Supported by the Royal Family:

The Royal Family actively align themselves with numerous charitable organizations, providing crucial support and lending their influential status to the causes they champion. One such organization is The Prince's Trust, founded by His Royal Highness Prince Charles. This charity aids disadvantaged young people by offering support in areas such as education, employment, and personal development. Additionally, The Duke and Duchess of Cambridge have devoted themselves to various mental health initiatives, such as Heads Together, which focuses on ending the stigma surrounding mental health and providing support to those affected. These are just a few examples of the many charitable organizations supported by the Royal Family, demonstrating their broad-ranging commitment to making a difference in diverse fields.

Raising Awareness and Generating Funds:

The Royal Family's involvement in charitable work goes beyond simply lending their names to causes; they actively engage in raising awareness and generate significant funds for the organizations they support. Their high public profile allows them to capture the attention of millions, shining a spotlight on important societal issues. The Royal Family utilizes their influence to encourage public donations, host fundraising events, and participate in charity walks, runs, and galas. Their efforts to mobilize support ensure that these organizations can continue their work on an increasingly larger scale, thus maximizing their impact.

Impact and Influence:

The Royal Family's charitable work has had a profound impact on communities both nationally and globally. By aligning themselves with various causes, they contribute to a significant positive change in numerous areas. For instance, in the field of mental health, the Royal Family's advocacy has helped break down societal barriers and encourage open discussions surrounding mental well-being. Their dedication to addressing homelessness has led to the establishment of shelters and initiatives that provide much-needed support to those in need. These are just a few instances where the influence of the Royal Family has led to tangible improvements in the lives of countless individuals.

THE CHARITABLE WORK of the British Royal Family is synonymous with their commitment to public service and making a positive impact on society. Their engagement in a broad array of causes, support for various charitable organizations, and efforts to raise awareness and funds highlight the extent of their dedication to improving the lives of others. The influence and impact of the Royal Family's charitable endeavors cannot be overstated – they have transformed countless lives, championed important causes, and continue to inspire individuals around the world to ensure a brighter future for all.

The Queen's Commonwealth

The foundations of the modern Commonwealth can be traced back to the Statute of Westminster in 1931, which established the constitutional framework for independent nations within the British Empire. Over time, this loose association of countries grew into the Commonwealth of Nations, formally established in 1949. With Queen Elizabeth II as its symbolic head, the Commonwealth operates on the principles of voluntary allegiance and mutual cooperation.

The Commonwealth serves as a platform for member nations to collaborate on economic, social, and political issues. Through forums such as the Commonwealth Heads of Government Meetings (CHOGM), member states engage in dialogue, exchange ideas, and work towards shared objectives. Whether it is promoting democratic governance, advancing human rights, or addressing climate change, the Commonwealth provides a forum where countries can voice their concerns, seek solutions, and collectively tackle global issues.

One of the remarkable strengths of the Commonwealth is its emphasis on inclusivity and diversity. Its membership spans continents, encompassing countries from Africa, Asia, the Americas, the Caribbean, Europe, and the Pacific. This wide-ranging representation ensures that a multitude of perspectives and experiences are brought to the table. By fostering cultural exchange and understanding, the Commonwealth promotes harmony amongst its members, fostering a sense of unity that transcends national boundaries.

The Commonwealth also champions youth empowerment and engagement, recognizing the importance of nurturing young leaders. The Commonwealth Youth Programme, launched in 1973, offers opportunities for young people to develop leadership skills, share their experiences, and contribute to meaningful change. The biennial Commonwealth Youth Forum provides a platform for young voices to be heard and their ideas incorporated into policy-making discussions. By investing in the next generation, the Commonwealth ensures a vibrant and sustainable future for its member nations.

Beyond the realm of politics and governance, the Commonwealth has made significant contributions to various sectors. The Commonwealth Games, held every four years, bring together athletes from member countries to compete in a spirit of friendly rivalry. This global sporting event not only showcases athletic prowess but also fosters cultural exchange and mutual understanding. The Commonwealth Fund for Technical Cooperation supports development projects across member nations, focusing on areas such as education, healthcare, and sustainable development. These initiatives help build capacity, promote economic growth, and address pressing social challenges.

Despite its achievements, the Commonwealth is not without its critics and challenges. Some argue that the association retains colonial legacies and perpetuates a hierarchical relationship, with the British monarchy at its center. However, the Commonwealth has evolved into a voluntary and egalitarian network of nations, where shared values and mutual respect form the bedrock of its existence. Moreover, the Commonwealth acknowledges and learns from its historical shortcomings, actively working towards reconciliation and inclusivity.

Looking to the future, the Queen's Commonwealth faces multiple opportunities and challenges. Given its global reach and diverse membership, the Commonwealth is well-positioned to play a significant role in addressing pressing global issues. Climate change, economic inequality, and the COVID-19 pandemic are just a few examples where the Commonwealth can facilitate collective action and cooperation. Furthermore, the Commonwealth's capacity to engage with emerging global powers, such as India and Nigeria, will shape its relevance and influence in the years to come. From its humble beginnings as an association of former British colonies, the Commonwealth has evolved into a global platform for dialogue, development, and shared values. By fostering youth empowerment, championing inclusivity, and addressing common challenges, the Commonwealth remains a vital force for positive change in an ever-changing world. The story of the Queen's Commonwealth is one of resilience, adaptability, and the enduring power of collective action.

Chapter 13: Royal Family Dynamics

THE QUEEN AND HER HEIRS

To begin exploring this topic, it is essential to understand the role of the Queen in the monarchy. Queen Elizabeth II, the current reigning monarch, has been on the throne since 1952, making her the longest-reigning monarch in British history. As the Queen, her responsibilities include representing the nation both domestically and internationally, ceremonial duties, and serving as a figurehead for the people of the United Kingdom and the Commonwealth.

One of the most intriguing aspects of the Queen's role is the question of succession. The British monarchy operates under the system of hereditary succession, meaning that the throne is passed down through the royal bloodline. This system has been in place for centuries and has ensured the continuity of the monarchy throughout history. However, in recent times, there have been discussions and debates surrounding the laws of succession, particularly in regard to gender equality and primogeniture.

The issue of gender equality within the royal succession process has been a contentious one. Historically, male heirs took precedence over their female counterparts, regardless of their age. This practice, known as male primogeniture, resulted in many instances where younger brothers were placed ahead of their older sisters in the line of succession. However, the British government took a significant step towards gender equality in 2013 with the passing of the Succession to the Crown Act. This act abolished male primogeniture, ensuring that the eldest child, regardless of gender, would inherit the throne. This change allowed Princess Charlotte, the second child of the Duke and Duchess of Cambridge, to maintain her position in the line of succession despite having a younger brother, Prince Louis.

The Queen's heirs are not limited to her immediate family. The line of succession extends beyond her children and grandchildren and encompasses a broader network of relatives. As of this writing, the direct heirs to the British throne are the Queen's eldest son, Prince Charles, followed by his two sons, Prince William and Prince Harry. Beyond them, the line of succession includes Prince William's three children - Prince George, Princess Charlotte, and Prince Louis.

The Queen and her heirs have undergone various challenges and changes throughout their lives. The role of the heir to the throne is not merely ceremonial; it also includes extensive training and preparation for the responsibilities they will one day assume. Prince Charles, as the Prince of Wales and the eldest son of the Queen, has been groomed for this role for many years. He has taken part in numerous engagements and royal duties, familiarizing himself with the intricacies of being the future King. Similarly, Prince William has accompanied his grandmother on official visits and engagements, slowly but steadily assuming a more prominent role as the second in line to the throne.

While the Queen is currently the longest-reigning monarch, eventually, there will be a transition of power. This transition will mark a significant moment in British history and will see the reign of a new monarch. With the preparations and grooming of the heirs, the transition is expected to be smooth, as the future King is already well-versed in the duties and responsibilities that await. The Queen's role as head of state and the intricate systems of hereditary succession are essential aspects to understand. The issue of gender equality and changes in the laws of succession have shaped the line of succession, ensuring that individuals are now considered based on their birth order, regardless of gender. The Queen's direct heirs, including her eldest son and his children, are preparing for their future roles as the inheritors of the throne. Despite the challenges and changes that come with the passing of time, the British monarchy continues to evolve, ensuring its longevity and stability for generations to come.

Sibling Relationships in the Royal Family

One aspect that distinguishes sibling relationships in the royal family is the significant age gaps often found between siblings. This age difference can create distinct dynamics within the family, as older siblings may act as role models or even parental figures to their younger counterparts. It also means that siblings may have vastly different life experiences and responsibilities, leading to a sense of disconnect or misunderstanding. For instance, in the British royal family, Prince Charles and his younger siblings, Princess Anne, Prince Andrew, and Prince Edward, have substantial age differences, with Charles being the eldest. This age gap has undoubtedly shaped their relationships, with Charles assuming a more prominent role within the family as the first in line to the throne.

Furthermore, sibling relationships in the royal family are inherently influenced by the hierarchical position of each individual. A clear example of this can be seen in the British royal family, where the line of succession determines the importance and public visibility of each sibling. The eldest sibling, as the direct heir to the throne, often carries significant responsibilities and garners more attention from the public and media. This hierarchical structure can sometimes lead to conflicts or rivalries among siblings, as they navigate their individual roles and positions within the family. However, it is important to note that the hierarchical position does not solely determine the nature of sibling relationships. Personal traits, upbringing, and individual choices also play a crucial role.

Shared experiences serve as another influential factor in sibling relationships within the royal family. Growing up in a unique environment, royals often face similar challenges and expectations that can foster a sense of camaraderie among siblings. From royal duties to public scrutiny and media intrusion, these shared experiences can create bonds that go beyond mere blood relations. In the British royal family, Princes William and Harry serve as an illustrative example. Their mother's tragic death, Princess Diana, and the subsequent media attention profoundly impacted their lives. This shared loss and the difficulties they faced in the limelight have showcased the strength of their sibling bond. Similarly, in other royal families, siblings may form strong alliances and support systems, relying on one another for guidance and empathy.

Despite the privileges and unique circumstances that come with being part of the royal family, sibling relationships within these dynasties are not immune to conflicts and tensions. Just like in any other family, disagreements can arise, and individuals may have different perspectives on various matters.

These conflicts, however, often occur under public scrutiny and can have significant repercussions. Media coverage and public perception can exacerbate family issues, making it challenging for siblings to resolve conflicts privately. Royal families must navigate these challenges while maintaining a united front, as their actions and interactions often reflect on the institution as a whole.

It is important to recognize that royal siblings are not only family members but also public figures. Their relationships, conflicts, and even affectionate moments are closely observed by the media and the public, who scrutinize every interaction, facial expression, and gesture. This constant spotlight places immense pressure on siblings to present themselves as a cohesive unit, reinforcing the image of stability and continuity that the monarchy seeks to uphold. While this pressure can strain sibling relationships, it also acts as a catalyst for siblings to find common ground and project a coordinated front, ensuring the longevity and public support of the institution. These relationships provide a unique lens through which we can understand the lives of those within the monarchy and the challenges they face. Despite the privilege and advantages that come with royal status, siblings within these families are not exempt from conflicts. However, they must navigate these conflicts under intense public scrutiny, influencing their interactions and the image they project to the world. Understanding the dynamics and complexities of sibling relationships in the royal family can shed light on the larger dynamics of monarchy and provide valuable insights into the personal lives of those who inhabit this unique world.

Chapter 14: The Influence of Royal Consorts

THE ROLE OF THE PRINCE Consort

When discussing the role of the Prince Consort, it is essential to emphasize their primary duty: supporting their spouse, the reigning queen. This support manifests in various ways, ranging from personal to public matters. In private, the Prince Consort contributes to the well-being and happiness of their spouse. They provide advice, companionship, and reassurance during the challenges and burdens of monarchical life. The Prince Consort is often the queen's confidant, offering a trustworthy and familiar presence amidst the regal responsibilities. This personal support is crucial for the monarch's emotional stability and overall effectiveness in their role as head of state.

In addition to their personal support, the Prince Consort is also deeply involved in public service. They engage in philanthropic work, champion important causes, and make notable contributions to society. One of the Prince Consort's significant responsibilities is acting as a patron or president of various charitable organizations. By utilizing their position and influence, Prince Consorts have the opportunity to raise awareness and funds for worthy causes, making a positive impact on communities and individuals in need. This involvement in charitable endeavors often earns the respect and admiration of the public, further enhancing the reputation of the monarchy.

Furthermore, the Prince Consort's role extends beyond domestic affairs; they are frequently engaged in diplomatic efforts on behalf of the monarch and the state. This involvement can range from formal state visits to attending international conferences. The Prince Consort's diplomatic engagements are vital for fostering relationships with foreign governments, promoting cultural exchange, and strengthening alliances. Their presence often signifies continuity and stability in bilateral relations, reinforcing the importance of diplomacy in modern governance.

In an era characterized by increased media exposure, the Prince Consort also plays a crucial role in shaping public opinion of the monarchy. With their participation in various events and ceremonies, they contribute to the monarchy's public image and, consequently, its reputation and support. The Prince Consort's demeanor, dress, and conduct influence the public perception of the monarchy and its relevance in contemporary society. Their involvement in public life, combined with the personal qualities they exemplify, can significantly impact the monarchy's popularity and public support.

It is important to note that the role of the Prince Consort is not static and has evolved over time. In earlier centuries, the role primarily revolved around providing heirs to the throne and ensuring the continuation of the dynasty. However, with the progression of society, the Prince Consort's role has expanded to encompass a much broader range of responsibilities. Today, they are expected to fulfill their duties with a combination of tradition and adaptation to the social, political, and cultural context of the times. Their personal support to the reigning queen is invaluable, providing emotional strength and guidance in the face of royal obligations. By actively participating in public service, the Prince Consort positively impacts society and raises the monarchy's standing. Their diplomatic engagements strengthen international relations and promote cultural exchange, while their conduct and involvement in public life shape public opinion of the monarchy.

The Queen's Consorts Through History

In ancient civilizations, the Queen's consort was often chosen based on political alliances and dynastic considerations. The role of these consorts was primarily to provide heirs and secure the continuity of the royal line. However, they also played an important social and ceremonial role, acting as a representative of the ruling Queen at public events and diplomatic affairs. In these ancient societies, such as ancient Egypt and Mesopotamia, the Queen's consort would often hold significant authority and wield substantial power in their own right.

One notable example of a Queen's consort from ancient history is the Pharaoh Akhenaten, who was the husband of the famous Queen Nefertiti.

Akhenaten broke with tradition by actively promoting a monotheistic religion centered around the sun god Aten. This radical departure from the polytheistic worship of Egypt's pantheon was heavily influenced by the Queen's consort and showcased their ability to shape the religious and cultural landscape of the time. Akhenaten's reign marked a pivotal moment in Egyptian history, highlighting the significance of the Queen's consort in shaping the destiny of an entire civilization.

Moving forward in time, we encounter the medieval era, where the role of the Queen's consort took on different dimensions. During this period, marriage alliances and political considerations remained essential factors in the selection of a Queen's consort. However, the consort's role expanded to include diplomatic negotiations, land management, and even mili

Chapter 15: The Monarchy and Colonialism

THE LEGACY OF THE BRITISH Empire

One of the most significant legacies of the British Empire is its contribution to the spread of the English language. English became the lingua franca of the British Empire, and it remains one of the most widely spoken languages in the world today. English has become the language of international diplomacy, business, and academia, facilitating global communication and understanding. Without the British Empire's influence, it is conceivable that the dominance of English would not have been as widespread, and the world would have developed a different linguistic landscape.

Economically, the legacy of the British Empire can be both positive and negative. The empire played a central role in the development of a globalized trade network, establishing colonies as sources of raw materials and markets for manufactured goods. The British Empire brought economic stability and infrastructure development to many regions, creating railways, ports, and other essential facilities. However, the economic benefits were not equally distributed, with the empire often extracting resources from its colonies without fair compensation. This economic exploitation left many former colonies economically disadvantaged and set the stage for lasting economic inequalities that persist to this day.

In terms of political legacy, the British Empire played a crucial role in shaping the systems of governance in its colonies. The empire introduced and established parliamentary democracy in many regions, leaving behind constitutional frameworks that continue to influence political systems. For example, India, the jewel in the crown of the British Empire, adopted Westminster-style democracy after gaining independence. However, the imposition of British rule also disrupted existing political structures and led to conflicts and tensions that are still evident in some post-colonial states. The legacy of the British Empire's political institutions is thus a complex mixture of progress and challenges, with the impact varying from country to country.

Culturally, the British Empire left an indelible mark on the world. The influence of British literature, art, music, and sports permeated throughout the empire, leaving a lasting imprint on the cultural identities of formerly colonized nations. This cultural exchange, however, was often one-sided, with the British Empire imposing its own cultural norms and values on the indigenous populations. The legacy of cultural imperialism and assimilation is a topic of ongoing debate and exploration today, as societies grapple with the effects of the British Empire's cultural legacy on their own identities and traditions.

Beyond these general legacies, it is essential to examine the specific experiences of individual countries within the British Empire to understand the full scope of its impact. For example, in Africa, the legacy of colonialism includes artificially drawn borders that continue to fuel ethnic conflicts, economic disparities, and governance challenges. The British Empire's divide-and-rule policies in India exacerbated religious and ethnic tensions, which ultimately led to the partition of the Indian subcontinent. The legacy of colonialism also left scars on indigenous communities, with histories of mistreatment, violence, and cultural erasure.

However, it is important to note that the legacy of the British Empire is not solely characterized by exploitation and suffering. The empire also played a role in the spread of education, technology, and infrastructure that laid the foundation for development in many countries. The British legal system, for example, is still used in many former colonies, providing a framework for justice and governance. The British Empire's advancements in healthcare and medicine also brought significant improvements to many regions, saving countless lives and improving public health. Its influence can be seen in the widespread use of the English language, the global economic order, political systems, cultural identities, and ongoing challenges faced by former colonies. While the empire brought about progress and development in some areas, it also left behind deep-rooted inequalities, conflicts, and cultural tensions. Understanding and addressing the legacy of the British Empire is essential for creating a more equitable and just world in the future.

Chapter 16: The Monarchy and the Military

THE ROYAL FAMILY'S Military Connections

Throughout history, the British Royal Family has maintained a deep connection with the military. This association can be traced back centuries and has played a significant role in shaping the monarchy's image as a symbol of national unity and stability. From serving on the frontline to supporting veterans and their families, the Royal Family's commitment to the armed forces is unwavering. In this one, we will explore the rich military heritage of the Royal Family, examining how they have served in the military, their involvement in military organizations, and their ongoing support for military personnel.

The Royal Family's military connections can be traced back to the very formation of the monarchy. The British Empire, at the height of its power, relied heavily on its military to expand its territories and protect its interests around the globe. Kings and queens would lead their armies into battle, symbolizing their devotion to the nation and their duty as the head of state. This tradition continues to this day, albeit in a more ceremonial role. The Royal Family's commitment to the armed forces is evident through the number of family members who have served in various branches of the military.

Perhaps one of the most prominent examples of the Royal Family's military service is Prince Philip, the Duke of Edinburgh. Born into the Greek and Danish royal families, Prince Philip fled with his family during the Greek-Turkish war. He later joined the British Royal Navy and served with distinction during World War II. Prince Philip's military career spanned over a decade, during which he saw action in the Mediterranean and the Pacific. His experience in the military shaped his character and instilled in him a deep sense of duty and loyalty that he carried throughout his life.

Prince Philip's military service is not an isolated example within the Royal Family. Prince Harry, the Duke of Sussex, also served in the armed forces, undertaking two tours of duty in Afghanistan. His dedication to the military and his service alongside his fellow soldiers earned him the respect and admiration of both his colleagues and the public. This connection to the military extended beyond his active service, as he went on to establish the Invictus Games, an international sporting event for wounded, injured, and sick servicemen and women.

The Royal Family's involvement in military organizations has also been significant. Over the years, they have taken on honorary roles in a wide range of military institutions, demonstrating their commitment to supporting the armed forces. For instance, Queen Elizabeth II holds the position of Colonel-in-Chief or Colonel of over 30 military units worldwide. This honorary role allows her to maintain a close relationship with the military and to support their activities through visits, ceremonies, and social engagements.

The Royal Family's military connections extend beyond one individual or even one generation. The Prince of Wales, Prince William, and Prince Harry are all actively involved in supporting military personnel and their families through various charitable initiatives. The Prince's Trust, founded by Prince Charles, has a dedicated program that provides support and guidance for veterans transitioning to civilian life. Similarly, the Duke and Duchess of Cambridge launched the Heads Together campaign, focusing on improving mental health support for current and former military personnel.

One cannot discuss the Royal Family's military connections without mentioning their involvement in Remembrance Day commemorations. Each year, the Royal Family pays tribute to the fallen by attending the Cenotaph ceremony in London and laying wreaths in honor of those who sacrificed their lives in conflicts around the world. This solemn occasion serves as a reminder of the Royal Family's profound empathy and respect for those who serve or have served in the armed forces. From their own military service to their involvement in military organizations and support for veterans, the Royal Family's commitment to the armed forces is deeply ingrained. Their associations with the military serve to reinforce the bond between the monarchy and the nation, symbolizing strength, tradition, and a shared honor.

As custodians of this rich heritage, the Royal Family continues to play an essential role in honoring and supporting the military and its personnel.

Chapter 17: The Royal Family and the Church

THE MONARCH AS HEAD of the Church of England

To fully understand why the Monarch is considered the Head of the Church of England, we must delve into the turbulent period of the English Reformation. In the early 16th century, England, like many other countries in Europe, was experiencing religious upheaval. The Catholic Church's authority was being challenged by the Protestant movement, and leaders such as Martin Luther and John Calvin were gaining popularity. King Henry VIII, in his quest for a male heir, sought to annul his marriage to Catherine of Aragon and marry Anne Boleyn, which the Pope refused to grant. This led Henry VIII to break with Rome and establish the Church of England, with himself as its head. This act not only allowed Henry to divorce and remarry, but it also marked the birth of a new religious institution under the control of the English monarch.

The role of the Monarch as the Head of the Church of England has endured for centuries, even as religious dynamics have evolved. The British monarch, regardless of their personal faith or lack thereof, is both a constitutional and religious figurehead. As the Supreme Governor of the Church, they hold significant influence over ecclesiastical matters and are responsible for appointing bishops, archbishops, and other high-ranking clergy. This role provides the Monarch with a unique position of authority in both the religious and the political realms. It is this intertwining of the monarchy and the Church that has shaped the identity of the British nation and its institutions.

One fascinating aspect of the Monarch's relationship with the Church is the coronation ceremony itself. During the coronation, the King or Queen takes an oath to uphold the laws and customs of the Church of England. This symbolic act emphasizes the Monarch's role as the defender and promoter of the Anglican faith. It also highlights the influence of religion on the monarchy's legitimacy and public perception. For centuries, the coronation has been a powerful source of national unity, blending religious and secular authority into one ceremonial event.

Despite its historical and cultural significance, the role of the Monarch as the Head of the Church of England has been a subject of debate and criticism. Some argue that it undermines the principle of religious freedom and promotes a form of religious discrimination. Others question the compatibility of this arrangement with a modern, diverse society. However, proponents of the monarchy argue that it provides a unifying force in a country with diverse religious beliefs, and that the Monarch's presence in the Church ensures its continued relevance and connection to the wider population.

In recent decades, as religious adherence has declined in the United Kingdom, the Monarch's role as the Head of the Church of England has raised further questions. With a growing population identifying as non-religious or belonging to other faiths, some argue that the monarchy should distance itself from a specific religious affiliation. This has led to discussions about the future of the relationship between the monarchy and the Church, and potential reforms that could be made to address these concerns. Ultimately, any significant changes would require careful consideration and likely involve constitutional amendments. From its origins in the English Reformation to its relevance in the modern era, this unique relationship has shaped the identity of the British monarchy and the Church itself. While discussions about its future continue, there is no doubt that the Monarch's role as the Head of the Church of England remains a central feature of the British constitutional and religious landscape.

Royal Weddings and Religious Ceremonies

Throughout history, royal weddings have been closely tied to religious ceremonies. Monarchical power often derived its legitimacy from a divine mandate, and marrying within the confines of religious traditions was a way to reinforce this connection. The wedding ceremony itself is a sacred moment, a union blessed by a higher power. By incorporating religious rites into royal weddings, monarchs sought to symbolize their divine right to rule and their commitment to upholding the religious values of their realm.

Religious ceremonies during royal weddings vary significantly depending on the traditions and customs of the nations involved. The rituals and practices can differ from country to country, reflecting the rich tapestry of global religious diversity. For example, in the United Kingdom, where Anglicanism is the established church, royal weddings typically take place in grand cathedrals or historic churches. The marriage vows are administered by a member of the clergy, and the ceremony includes prayers, scripture readings, and hymns. These religious elements infuse the event with a solemnity and reverence befitting the union of a future king or queen.

In some cases, royal weddings can also bridge different religious traditions. When a member of a royal family marries a person of a different faith, careful consideration is given to ensure the inclusion and respect of both religious backgrounds. This often involves the presence of multiple religious leaders and the incorporation of rituals from both traditions. These interfaith ceremonies not only promote a spirit of inclusivity but also reflect the multicultural and diverse nature of modern society.

Beyond their religious significance, royal weddings have broader societal implications. They act as a unifying force, bringing people together in celebrations that transcend national divides. These weddings captivate the collective imagination, offering a sense of escapism and a temporary reprieve from daily concerns. They become cultural touchstones, generating national pride and a sense of shared identity. Whether watching from afar or participating in public festivities, people feel a deep connection to these joyous occasions that mark a new one in the lives of their beloved royal figures.

Furthermore, the media plays a crucial role in disseminating information and creating a global dialogue surrounding royal weddings and religious ceremonies. Journalists and photographers capture every detail, from the bride's dress to the exchange of rings, providing millions of people with a front-row seat to these momentous events. The media frenzy surrounding royal weddings not only fuels public interest but also shapes public perception. It is through these channels that societies learn about the nuances of different religious practices and gain a deeper understanding of the cultural significance of royal nuptials.

In recent years, royal weddings have also witnessed a gradual evolution, reflecting shifting societal values and expectations. Couples are incorporating more personal touches into their ceremonies, melding traditions with contemporary elements that reflect their identities and aspirations. This blending of the old and the new serves as a reminder of the enduring nature of religious traditions while embracing the ever-changing nature of the world we live in. By doing so, royal couples inspire others to celebrate their own unique unions and honor their religious heritage in creative and meaningful ways. They represent the merging of divine and worldly spheres, creating a space where religious heritage and royal lineage intersect. These grand occasions captivate the imagination and provide a sense of collective celebration and national pride. As we explore the fascinating world of royal weddings and religious ceremonies, we will uncover the rich tapestry of human culture and the diverse ways in which societies honor love, devotion, and tradition.

Chapter 18: The Royal Family and the Environment

THE ROYAL PARKS AND Gardens

London's Royal Parks and Gardens boast a storied past dating back centuries, rooted in a regal legacy that continues to shape their essence and purpose. It was during the reign of Henry VIII that the concept of royal parks gained prominence, with the documentary evidence of his hunting activities in the 1530s serving as a testament to this fact. Over time, these parks transformed into expressions of power, wealth, and prestige—a representation of the monarchy's dominion over nature. Each park holds unique stories and architectural remnants that reflect the priorities and tastes of different monarchs, from the grandeur of St James's Park designed by King Henry VIII himself, to the elegance of Kensington Gardens cherished by Queen Victoria and Prince Albert. These historical layers contribute to the allure and enchantment of the Royal Parks and Gardens, making them truly remarkable cultural assets.

Beyond their historical significance, the Royal Parks and Gardens are invaluable for their contribution to environmental sustainability. In the face of urbanization and the challenges posed by climate change, these green spaces act as crucial lungs for the city, purifying the air and providing a habitat for a wealth of flora and fauna. London is not only a global financial hub but also a biodiversity hotspot with over 1,300 species of plants and 400 species of birds recorded within the city. The Royal Parks, serving as sanctuaries for wildlife, play a pivotal role in preserving this rich biodiversity. Furthermore, their trees help mitigate the impacts of climate change, acting as carbon sinks, reducing the heat island effect, and providing shade during the scorching summer months. By nurturing native plants and encouraging sustainable management practices, the Royal Parks and Gardens exemplify the urgent need for urban green spaces in an era of rapid urbanization.

In addition to their cultural and environmental significance, the Royal Parks and Gardens offer immense recreational value and contribute to the wellbeing of London's residents and visitors. With picturesque landscapes, meandering paths, and inviting lawns, these spaces provide a peaceful respite from the hustle and bustle of city life, accommodating a multitude of activities. Families gather for picnics, children delight in playgrounds, and friends engage in sports, fostering social connections and promoting healthy lifestyles. Moreover, the Royal Parks and Gardens are a haven for joggers and walkers, offering rejuvenating opportunities for exercise and recreation in the heart of the city. Research has shown that spending time in green spaces has a profound positive impact on mental health, reducing stress, improving mood, and enhancing cognitive function. Therefore, the Royal Parks and Gardens truly serve as natural therapy amidst the urban chaos, inviting people to replenish their spirits and find solace in the embrace of nature.

Efforts to preserve and enhance the Royal Parks and Gardens are a testament to the commitment of both the governmental authorities and the broader community. The Royal Parks charity, responsible for managing and maintaining these green spaces, plays a vital role in ensuring their continued existence and accessibility for all. The charity engages in horticultural initiatives, educational programs, and conservation projects to safeguard the natural and cultural assets of these parks. Volunteers, local community groups, and organizations also actively participate in various activities, from wildlife monitoring to community gardening, contributing to the sense of ownership and promoting community cohesion. Through collaborative efforts, the Royal Parks and Gardens are not only preserved for future generations but are also evolving hubs of dynamic engagement, ensuring their relevance in a changing world.

As we conclude this one, we are reminded of the immense significance and multifaceted nature of London's Royal Parks and Gardens. They are not simply patches of greenery, but living testimonies to the city's heritage, champions of environmental sustainability, and sanctuaries of wellbeing. The Royal Parks and Gardens have the power to delight, inspire, and heal, offering a resplendent and harmonious tapestry woven into the fabric of London. As guardians of these treasured green spaces, it is our collective responsibility to ensure their continued preservation and promotion, allowing them to flourish as everlasting symbols of the city's natural and cultural heritage.

Chapter 19: The Personal Lives of Royal Family Members

LOVE AND MARRIAGE IN the Royal Family

The lives of royalty are often viewed through a lens of glamour and pageantry, with their relationships under constant scrutiny. However, behind the grandeur, there are real people navigating the complexities of love and marriage just like anyone else. In this book, we will take a closer look at the dynamics of love and marriage within the Royal Family, examining historical perspectives, modern-day realities, and the challenges faced by those who choose to tie the knot within this prestigious institution.

A Historical Perspective

To understand love and marriage in the Royal Family, it is important to delve into the historical context. Throughout the centuries, royal marriages were often strategic alliances, aimed at forging political alliances or strengthening dynasties. Affection and individual choice were rarely prioritized, and love matches were often discouraged. Royal individuals were expected to prioritize duty and the best interests of their kingdom over personal feelings. As a result, many royal marriages were arranged, leading to potential challenges when it came to fostering genuine love and compatibility.

Modern-day Realities

In the modern era, love and marriage within the Royal Family have seen significant changes. The shift towards personal choice and genuine affection has become more prominent. Prince Albert and Queen Victoria marked a turning point in the attitude towards love in the Royal Family, sharing a deeply affectionate and passionate marriage. With the passing of time, royal individuals have been given more freedom to choose their own partners, although still subjected to certain expectations and considerations. This one explores some noteworthy examples of love matches within the Royal Family, shedding light on the evolving attitudes towards marriage.

Challenges and Contradictions

While love and marriage are aspirations that bind people across cultures and backgrounds, the royal platform presents unique challenges. Balancing personal desires with the expectations of the crown can be an intricate dance. From public scrutiny to the pressures of maintaining the reputation of the monarchy, royal couples must navigate a complex web of responsibilities. This one delves into the challenges faced by royal individuals in maintaining successful marriages, and how the pressures of monarchy can both solidify and strain their relationships.

Love Across Borders

In the modern era, love in the Royal Family often transcends national borders. Marriages between royals from different countries can lead to a merging of cultures, while also raising questions about loyalty and divided identities. This one examines relationships within the Royal Family that have crossed geographical boundaries, exploring how love can transcend borders and contribute to greater understanding and harmony between nations.

The Role of Love in Monarchy

While love may be a central theme in marriage, its role in the context of monarchy is somewhat different. In addition to personal fulfillment, royal unions must consider the broader implications for the monarchy and the nation. Stability, continuity, and representation of tradition are crucial factors. This one explores the delicate balance between personal happiness and the responsibilities that accompany royal titles, shedding light on the ways in which love and marriage can influence the monarchy itself.

Lessons Learned

Throughout history, love and marriage in the Royal Family have provided valuable lessons for individuals within and outside the realm of royalty. The stories of successful and unsuccessful unions serve as cautionary tales and sources of inspiration. This final one summarizes the key lessons learned from the experiences of the Royal Family, offering insights into how their struggles and triumphs can inform our own approach to love and marriage.

LOVE AND MARRIAGE IN the Royal Family provide captivating narratives that speak to the complexities of relationships within the realm of monarchy. Through a historical lens, we grasp the transformation from strategic alliances towards love matches. Nonetheless, this transition does not exempt royal individuals from facing unique challenges and pressures. Love transcends borders and can contribute to greater understanding between nations. However, it must be balanced with the responsibilities of monarchy. By examining these themes, we can extract valuable lessons from the lives of the Royal Family and apply them to our own understanding of love and marriage.

The Tragedies and Triumphs of Royal Life

Royal life has always fascinated and captivated societies throughout history. From the grandeur of palaces to the splendor of royal ceremonies, the lives of monarchs have long been a subject of both admiration and intrigue. However, beneath the pomp and circumstance lie tales of tragedy and triumph that shed light on the complexities and challenges associated with being a member of a royal family. This book aims to explore the multifaceted nature of royal life, delving into the triumphs and tragedies that have shaped the course of history and offer a deeper understanding of the human experience within the confines of royalty.

The Heir's Burden

The term "royal succession" often evokes images of joyful announcements and celebrations, marking the passing of power from one generation to the next. However, behind this seemingly joyous process lies a burden that weighs heavily on the heir. The responsibility of carrying on a centuries-old legacy, combined with the pressure to meet lofty expectations, can create a formidable challenge. In this one, we will delve into the triumphs and tragedies experienced by heirs throughout history, highlighting the struggles they face in reconciling their individuality with the weight of tradition.

Duty and Sacrifice: The Regal Role

Royalty is more than just a title; it is a calling that demands self-sacrifice and endless devotion to duty. Monarchs are not merely figureheads; they embody the aspirations and identity of their nation. This one will examine the triumphs and tragedies that arise from the regal role. From the external challenges of political crises to internal battles with personal desires and sacrifices, we will explore the hardships faced by those who bear the crown, shedding light on the hidden toll that duty takes on their lives.

Love and Tragedy in Royal Marriages

Marriage has long been a strategic tool used by royal families to solidify alliances and maintain their lineage. However, the pursuit of love and personal happiness often clashes with the demands of statecraft. In this one, we will explore the triumphs and tragedies that have occurred within royal marriages. From epic love stories that defy societal expectations to scandalous affairs that threaten the stability of kingdoms, we will uncover the delicate balance between personal desires and royal obligations within the framework of matrimony.

Behind the Curtains: The Tragedies of Intrigue and Power

Behind the glamorous façade of royal life exists a world of ruthless power struggles, dangerous intrigues, and deadly conspiracies. This one will delve into the triumphs and tragedies of royal courts, exploring the cutthroat nature of palace politics and its consequences for those entangled within. From the backstabbing maneuverings of ambitious courtiers to the tragic ends of those who dared to challenge the established order, we will uncover the darker side of royal life.

Adaptation and Resilience: The Triumphs of Modern Royalty

The modern era presents new challenges for royal families as they navigate an ever-changing world. This one will highlight the triumphs of adaptation and resilience, exploring how royal families have managed to retain their relevance and significance in contemporary societies. From embracing progressive causes to forging connections with their subjects, we will examine the strategies employed by modern monarchs to secure their place in an evolving world.

THE TRAGEDIES AND TRIUMPHS of royal life are a testament to the complexity and humanity of those who occupy these gilded positions. The burden of succession, the sacrifices of duty, the trials of love, the intrigues of power, and the ability to adapt and overcome are themes that resonate throughout history. By exploring these facets of royal life, we gain a greater understanding of the universal struggles faced by individuals in positions of power and influence. In shedding light on these triumphs and tragedies, we hope to provide a comprehensive examination of the human experience within the realm of royalty.

Chapter 20: Conclusion

THE ENDURING LEGACY of British Royalty

With a rich tapestry of traditions, ceremonies, and myths, the British monarchy has endured for centuries, its legacy extending far beyond the borders of the United Kingdom. From influencing fashion trends to serving as historical figureheads, the British royal family has left an indelible mark on society, shaping culture, politics, and even the global perception of power and elegance. In this essay, we will delve into the enduring legacy of British royalty, exploring its significance in an ever-evolving world and the fascination it continues to inspire in people worldwide.

1. Cultural Significance:

Starting with the overarching cultural significance, it is undeniable that the British royals have played a pivotal role in shaping and defining British culture. The monarchy's time-honored traditions, such as Trooping the Colour or the Changing of the Guard, have become iconic symbols of the nation's identity. These events, steeped in history and spectacle, serve not only as national rituals but also as tourist attractions, drawing millions of visitors from around the world each year. Their long-standing association with noble values, dignity, and stability reinforces the idea of the monarchy as a cornerstone of British society.

Moreover, the British royal family's patronage of the arts and charitable initiatives has greatly contributed to the growth and preservation of cultural heritage. The Royal Collection, comprising a vast array of artworks and historic artifacts, provides a tangible testament to the influence of monarchy in the realm of visual arts. Their support of charitable organizations, spearheaded by prominent figures such as the late Princess Diana, has helped raise awareness about numerous social issues, lending a compassionate touch to the seemingly distant institution.

2. Diplomatic Role:

Beyond its domestic influence, British royalty has played a significant diplomatic role throughout history, shaping the nation's relationships with other countries. The monarchy serves as a symbol of continuity and stability, allowing for the preservation of age-old alliances and the development of new ones. State visits by the Queen and other members of the royal family help forge stronger ties with international partners and showcase the United Kingdom's soft power on the global stage.

The Queen's Commonwealth connections, for example, provide a unique platform for diplomatic and cultural exchange among the diverse nations within the Commonwealth of Nations. This network, comprising countries spanning continents, underscores the longevity and adaptability of the British monarchy as a unifying force. The royal family's ability to transcend political differences and foster relationships based on shared history and values has proven invaluable in maintaining diplomatic rapport.

3. Impact on Tourism:

Another facet of the enduring legacy of British royalty lies in its profound impact on tourism. One cannot underestimate the allure of visiting royal residences, such as Buckingham Palace, Windsor Castle, or Balmoral Castle, which are steeped in history, elegance, and grandeur. The fascination with the British royal family draws millions of tourists each year, generating significant revenue and driving the local economy.

The tourism industry surrounding royal landmarks and events extends far beyond the United Kingdom. The marriage of Prince William and Kate Middleton, for instance, attracted global attention and generated immense interest in the country, boosting tourism and fostering a sense of goodwill towards the British nation. The iconic image of British royalty, coupled with the spectacle of high-profile events, perpetuates the image of the United Kingdom as a land of majesty and refinement.

4. Influences on Fashion and Style:

Another enduring aspect of British royalty is its influence on fashion and style. Throughout the centuries, members of the royal family have served as trend-setters, dictating fashion choices and propelling designers into the spotlight. From Queen Elizabeth I's elaborate gowns to Princess Diana's modern yet elegant ensembles, the royal wardrobe has inspired countless individuals and designers alike.

The notoriety of the British royal family, combined with their access to the world's leading fashion houses, has fueled the global fascination with their style. From their choice of hats to jewelry, each fashion choice is meticulously scrutinized and often emulated. This enduring presence in the fashion world serves as a continuous reminder of the monarchy's longstanding connection with elegance and poise. From its cultural significance to the diplomatic role it plays, the British royal family's influence extends well beyond ceremonial duties and national pride. The impact on tourism, fashion, and the preservation of cultural heritage is evidence of the global appeal and ongoing relevance of this ancient institution. In an ever-changing world, the British monarchy remains a symbol of continuity, grace, and the enduring power of tradition.

Looking to the Future: Challenges and Opportunities

Looking to the future, it is natural for us to ponder the challenges and opportunities that lie ahead. As the world continues to evolve, so do the complexities we face. In this book, we will delve into these challenges and opportunities, exploring how they impact various aspects of our lives. By adopting a professional and academic tone, we aim to provide an approachable and friendly guide that generates discussions, enlightens readers, and stimulates thought about what lies ahead.

Technological Advancements: A Double-Edged Sword

The rapid pace of technological advancements presents both challenges and opportunities for society. On one hand, breakthroughs in fields such as artificial intelligence and automation promise improved efficiency and convenience. However, these advancements also bring concerns about job displacement and ethical considerations. As we explore the future, we must carefully navigate these waters, harnessing the power of technology while mitigating its potential negative impacts.

Climate Change: The Urgency of Action

One of the most pressing challenges we face is the increasingly alarming issue of climate change. As temperatures rise and extreme weather events become more frequent, we must address this crisis decisively. The future holds both challenges in adapting to a changing climate and opportunities in embracing renewable energy and sustainable practices. To protect our planet and secure a livable future, collaboration and transformative action are essential.

Globalization and Interconnectedness: A World Without Borders

The world continues to shrink as globalization and technological connectivity enable unprecedented levels of international interaction. While this brings tremendous opportunities for widespread collaboration and cross-cultural understanding, it also exposes us to new challenges. We must grapple with issues like income inequality, profound cultural changes, and the need for robust global governance structures. As we look to the future, embracing the benefits of interconnectedness while addressing its associated challenges will be crucial.

Demographic Shifts: Aging Populations and Changing Dynamics

Demographic shifts are reshaping societies around the world. As life expectancies rise and fertility rates decline, many nations are facing aging populations. This trend poses challenges in terms of healthcare systems, social welfare, and labor markets. However, it also presents opportunities for innovation in elder care, knowledge sharing between generations, and the reimagining of social structures. By adapting to these changes, we can create inclusive communities that thrive in the face of demographic transformations.

Education and Lifelong Learning: Preparing for an Ever-Changing World

In an era of rapid change, the ability to adapt and acquire new skills is crucial. Education and lifelong learning are becoming increasingly essential for individuals to stay relevant in a dynamic job market. The future demands innovative approaches to education, skill development, and upskilling opportunities. By investing in educational initiatives and embracing continuous learning, we can equip individuals with the tools needed to face both the challenges and opportunities of tomorrow.

Resilience and Adaptability: Navigating Uncertainty

The future is uncertain, and our ability to adapt and respond is crucial for success. Challenges such as pandemics, economic crises, and geopolitical shifts require resilience and agility. However, by embracing change and adopting a proactive mindset, we can transform these challenges into opportunities for growth. Whether it be through creating adaptable business models or fostering personal resilience, navigating uncertainty becomes a skill of paramount importance in the face of future challenges.

LOOKING TO THE FUTURE, we recognize that challenges and opportunities lie ahead in various realms of our lives. Technological advancements, climate change, globalization, demographic shifts, education, and resilience all shape the landscape we will encounter. While these challenges may seem daunting, it is essential to approach them with optimism and a drive for transformative action. By acknowledging the potential pitfalls and embracing the opportunities, we can forge a better future for ourselves and future generations. Let us embark on this journey together, ready to face the challenges head-on and seize the opportunities that await us.

www.ingramcontent.com/pod-product-compliance
Lightning Source LLC
Chambersburg PA
CBHW070916160726
48004CB00003B/1399